S   D

F O   R S™

BY JEFF FALLOW

2055
(941.1)

Writers and Readers Publishing, Inc.
P.O. Box 461, Village Station
New York, NY 10014

Writers and Readers Limited
35 Britannia Row
London N1 8QH
Tel: 0171 226 2522
Fax: 0171 359 1406
e-mail: begin@writersandreaders.com

First Published by Writers and Readers 1999
Text Copyright © Jeff Fallow
Illustration Copyright © Jeff Fallow
Cover Design: Jeff Fallow
Book Design: Emma Byrne

A Writers and Readers Documentary Comic Book
Copyright © 1999
ISBN # 0-86316-264-9
1 2 3 4 5 6 7 8 9 0

Printed in Finland by WSOY

Beginners Documentary Comic Books are published by Writers and Readers Publishing, Inc. Its trademark, consisting of the words "For Beginners, Writers and Readers Documentary Comic Books" and the Writers and Readers logo, is registered in the U. S. Patent and Trademark Office and in other countries.

Writers and Readers

publishing FOR BEGINNERS™ books continuously since 1975
1975:Cuba •1976: Marx •1977: Lenin •1978: Nuclear Power •1979: Einstein •Freud •1980: Mao • Trotsky •1981: Capitalism •1982: Darwin• Economics •French Revolution• Marx's Kapital •Food •Ecology •1983: DNA•Ireland •1984: London •Peace •Medicine •Orwell •Reagan • Nicaragua • Black History • 1985: Marx's Diary • 1986: Zen • Psychiatry • Reich • Socialism •Computers •Brecht •Elvis •1988: Architecture •Sex •JFK • Virginia Woolf• 1990: Nietzsche• Plato • Malcolm X • Judaism • 1991: WWII • Erotica • African History •1992: Philosophy • •Rainforests•Miles Davis •Islam• Pan Africanism •1993: Black Women • Arabs and Israel •1994: Babies • Foucault • Heidegger • Hemingway•Classical Music • 1995: Jazz •Jewish Holocaust • Health Care • Domestic Violence •Sartre • United Nations •Black Holocaust •Black Panthers • Martial Arts •History of Clowns •1996: Opera •Biology •Saussure •UNICEF •Kierkegaard •Addiction & Recovery •I Ching • Buddha •Derrida •Chomsky • McLuhan •Jung •1997: Lacan •Shakespeare • Structuralism •Che •1998:Fanon •Adler •Marilyn •Postmodernism •Cinema

contents

July 1, 1999: the return of a Scottish parliament in Edinburgh after almost 300 years. A turning-point in history, direct rule from London no longer a viable option for the future.

For most of its history, Scotland was an independent country, a separate European nation with its own economy and foreign policy, its own monarchy and armed forces. After the Act of Union in 1707, when Scotland became part of Great Britain, the Scots immediately became a minority.

But a demand for self-government has always existed since then (though more strongly at certain periods than at others) and, in a referendum held in September 1997, the majority of Scottish voters expressed their demand for the restoration of a Scottish parliament. The Scottish general election (Scotland's first EVER by universal suffrage) for Members of the Scottish Parliament would take place in May 1999.

Is this because of an anti-English sentiment? A resentment towards the English because they have tried in the past to conquer Scotland? Or because they have often taken (or been given) the credit for Scotland's achievements? Or because Scotland continues ultimately to be ruled from England?

Actually, no.

BBC NATIONAL NEWS

STRIKE ON THE LONDON UNDERGROUND... BLAH BLAH ... ENGLAND IN THE WORLD CUP... BLAH BLAH...

The issue is really about democracy, social justice, human rights and the decentralisation of power, not some narrow 'us and them' mentality.

However, national (not racial) awareness plays an important role. Swallowed up in the British state, Scotland has had to struggle to keep its national identity. 'National' news has traditionally meant British, or even London news (such as a strike on the underground), whereas Scottish affairs were seen as merely regional or local. From a British national viewpoint, the country's two main political parties are Labour and Conservative. In Scotland, the picture is different, the two main national parties being Labour and the SNP (Scottish National Party).

BBC SCOTLAND REGIONAL NEWS

THE SCOTTISH PARLIAMENT TODAY DECIDED TO GET RID OF ALL NUCLEAR WEAPONS IN SCOTLAND IN A MOVE TOWARDS WORLD PEACE. "DREAM ON", SAID THE DEFENCE MINISTER IN WHITEHALL.

To understand this, we must look at Scotland's history. So, without further ado, let us meet **SCOTLAND**, the nation that has given so much to the world yet has rarely recieved the credit...

AH YES. SCOTLAND'S ACHIEVEMENTS ... GOLF, WHISKY, HAGGIS, PORRIDGE, TARTAN, BAGPIPES. THAT SORT OF THING.

WELL, NO ACTUALLY. A WEE BIT MORE THAN THAT...

AS A NATION,
SCOTLAND'S HISTORY
BEGINS IN THE

DARK
AGES

Before that lies the
history of the land and
it's peoples BEFORE
it became Scotland.

So first, a quick PREhistory.

Geological evidence shows that the oldest rocks in Scotland (over 500 million years old) date from when the Southern Uplands (the present-day hills near the border with England) formed part of the bottom of the sea. A mere 200 million years after this time, carboniferous forest - 'coal swamps' - covered what are now the Central Lowlands with trees reaching 100ft tall whose trunks fossilized into coal. Here, giant amphibians lived, such as Crassigyrinus Scoticus, discovered near present-day Cowdenbeath, Fife.

TEMNOSPONDYL

CRASSIGYRINUS SCOTICU

Mineral oil, a more important fossil fuel today because of its many applications, derivatives and by-products, was formed by the heating and pressurising of chemicals below the North Sea floor, and is now Scotland's - indeed Britain's - main natural resource and a most important source of national income.

Control of this resource is a crucial political issue, which we shall come to later.

STETHACANTHUS ('BEARSDEN SHARK') - 300 MILLION YEARS AGO.

Dinosaur and other reptile fossils, such as Ornithosuchus, dating from the Age of Reptiles (100-300 million years ago), have been found throughout Scotland.

ELGINIA

STAGINOLEPIS

RNITHOSUCHUS

Volcanic upheaval followed, pushing up the Highlands from their beds of sedimentary mud. The last great series of eruptions ended about 40 million years ago. The four ice ages which followed shaped the Scotland we know today. The great ice sheets, ebbing and flowing as the climate warmed or cooled, cut through the rocks (forming the glens or valleys) and melted into lochs (lakes).

After the last Ice Age ended c.10,000 years ago, the land became forested, populated with moose, lynx, beaver, wolf and bear (all now extinct in Scotland). The first human beings arrived in Scotland between 9000 and 6000 BC. They were Mesolithic (Middle Stone Age) hunters, arriving from southern Britain and Ireland. At first they only visited during the summer months, not staying for the harsh Scottish winter, but they finally settled permanently.

They originally lived in caves such as Wemyss caves near Buckhaven, Fife, but eventually built circular stone houses. They survived on deer, wild boar, fish, shellfish and (occasionally) washed-up whale, always living in coastal areas, or along the courses of major rivers such as the Clyde, since the interior forest appeared mysterious and dangerous.

Meanwhile farming, which began in the Middle East about 8000 years ago, slowly spread across Europe. Between 4500 BC and 3000 BC Neolithic farmers arrived from continental Europe (some from the Baltic, others from the Mediterranean). They introduced barley, wheat, rye and domestic sheep and cattle, ending the need for a nomadic hunter's existence. At Skara Brae, Orkney, an entire Stone Age village is preserved, buried under drifted sand for centuries and now exposed in perfect condition, complete with stone furniture. The inhabitants wore clothes of sewn hide and fired pottery in peat fires. Other people meanwhile lived in crannogs, lake dwellings built on artificial islands or piers, such as at Bishop Loch, near Glasgow. The loch offered a natural defence as well as a food supply.

During the 2nd millennium BC, the Beaker People (so called because of their practice of burying earthenware beakers along with their dead) arrived from the Iberian peninsula, settling throughout Europe. They built great stone circles or henges throughout Britain, notably Stonehenge in England and, in Scotland, the Callanish circle on the Isle of Lewis, probably relatively soon after the beginning of the millennium.

As well as centres of religious ceremony and ritual magic, stone circles were also astronomical observatories; specially positioned for observing the movement of the sun and moon, seasons and equinoxes could be calculated - important to a farming society.

The Stone Age gave way to the Bronze Age (c.2000-500 BC), when the Celts arrived, originally from central Europe, and to the Iron Age (500 BC-AD 80, with the arrival of the Romans). Metal was now the chief material used for tools and weapons. The Celtic peoples in Scotland included the Picts in the north (probably so called because they painted pictures on their bodies before going to battle) and Britons in the south.

The Romans, advancing northwards through Britannia, found a land of fierce Pictish tribes and northern Britons, whom they collectively labelled 'Caledonii'. About AD 80, Gnaeus Julius Agricola (AD 37-93) decided to invade Caledonia. Governor of Britannia AD 78-85, Agricola was successor to Suetonius Paulinus, first Governor, who had subdued the anti-Roman revolt in the south east of England led by Queen Boudicca. Agricola defeated a united Caledonian army, commanded by Pictish king Calgacus, at the **Battle of Mons Graupius** (AD 84), whose exact site is unknown. Agricola's son-in-law Tacitus, a gifted writer, afterwards wrote an account of the battle, in which he imagines Calgacus telling his people 'They create a desert and call it peace!'.

JULIUS AGRICOLA

However, the Romans ultimately failed to subdue the Caledonii. With troops required more urgently in Europe to deal with hostilities in Germany, they retreated southwards, building **Hadrian's Wall** from the Solway to the Tyne, separating Caledonia from Roman-occupied Britannia and the rest of the Roman Empire.

Possibly a marked frontier rather than a defence, the wall now lies just south of the modern Scottish-English border. Yet the wall would form a traditional national boundary dividing the peoples to its north from their southern neighbours. (Today, Hadrian's Wall is more psychological than physical, but let's not digress.)

THE ROMANS LEFT THEIR MARK.
SCOTLAND'S NATIONAL HISTORY NOW BEGINS IN THE DARK AGES

When the Roman Empire collapsed, destroyed from outside by invasions of Gothic tribes and from inside by corruption and disunity, Europe entered the Dark Ages, when the European peoples formed themselves into a multitude of tiny feudal kingdoms, fighting each other for survival, control or territory. Without the 'protection' of Roman troops, weaker tribes were exposed to conquest by new masters, who in their turn would be subdued by even stronger nations.

The Dark Ages (5th-10th centuries AD) were so called because it was a period of intellectual 'darkness', i.e. lacking the 'light' or enlightenment of scientific knowledge, art and literature. Only monks of the Christian church, preserving and copying Greek and Roman texts, could read and write. Divided into so many small, warring kingdoms, Europe lacked the political stability or civil peace necessary for a network of large schools and universities.

The **SCOTS**, Gaelic-speaking invaders from Ireland, formed a kingdom on the West coast called Dalriada when their king, **Fergus Mor**, son of Eric, established a seat of power there around AD 500. Later, in AD 843, King **Kenneth MacAlpin** of Dalriada (whose father had perhaps married a Pictish princess) conquered the Picts, calling the newly united country Alba or SCOTLAND and becoming Kenneth I of Scotland. By 960, the Scottish kings ruled from Edinburgh, (though they were peripatetic until the 15th and 16th centuries) having conquered the Angles there, acquiring Lothian and the south east of Scotland.

The Angles, originally from Germany and arriving in the 5th century, had already been weakened by Norse (Viking) attacks. In 1034, Strathclyde (south-west Scotland) was acquired after the death of its king, Scotland's **Malcolm II** having won a decisive victory at Carham (near Coldstream in the south east) 16 years before. The islands remained under Norse control for a long time yet. The Western isles remained so until 1266, the Orkneys and the Shetlands until 1468-69, so that by the Middle Ages Scotland, like England and most of the European countries we are familiar with today, had become formed into a recognisable nation-state.

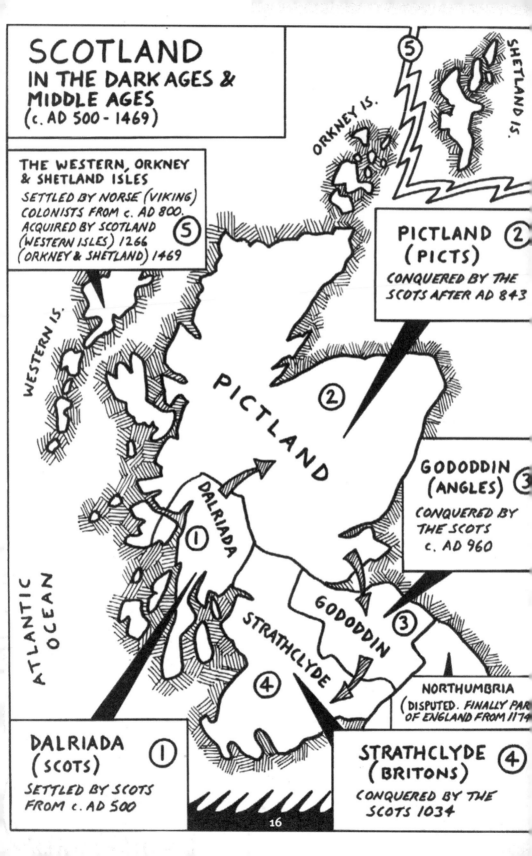

SCOTLAND
IN THE DARK AGES & MIDDLE AGES
(c. AD 500 - 1469)

THE WESTERN, ORKNEY & SHETLAND ISLES

SETTLED BY NORSE (VIKING) COLONISTS FROM c. AD 800. ACQUIRED BY SCOTLAND (WESTERN ISLES) 1266 (ORKNEY & SHETLAND) 1469 ⑤

ORKNEY IS.

SHETLAND IS.

⑤

PICTLAND (PICTS) ②

CONQUERED BY THE SCOTS AFTER AD 843

WESTERN IS.

PICTLAND

②

GODODDIN (ANGLES) ③

CONQUERED BY THE SCOTS c. AD 960

DALRIADA

①

GODODDIN

③

ATLANTIC OCEAN

STRATHCLYDE

GODODDIN

④

NORTHUMBRIA

(DISPUTED. FINALLY PART OF ENGLAND FROM 1174

DALRIADA (SCOTS) ①

SETTLED BY SCOTS FROM c. AD 500

STRATHCLYDE (BRITONS) ④

CONQUERED BY THE SCOTS 1034

16

Meanwhile, Christian religion helped unite the four peoples - Scots, Angles, Picts and Britons - culturally.
Missionary monks, notably St Ninian, St Mungo and St Columba, had converted them

to Christianity. The early Celtic church demanded poverty of its clergy, who lived as community monks (called 'culdees') among the ordinary people. **St Columba** established a monastery at Iona c. AD 570 which became an important centre of learning, though the monks lived in humble stone and turf shelters. From the mid 7th century, the Celtic church was gradually brought into line with the Roman Catholic orthodoxy of the rest of Western Europe.

But as Scottish kings extended their control southwards and English kings northwards, border disputes arose.

'There they will read about the thirsting pride
By which the Scot and Englishman are maddened,
Neither content to stay within his bounds'.

DANTE, *Paradiso*

Larger and more populous, England was the stronger kingdom, and defeat in battle for Scotland repeatedly meant having to pay feudal homage to the English crown, i.e. the Scottish king would have to accept the English king as overlord. Defeat for England, however, did not mean a reversal of the relationship between the two countries, only that England would try harder next time.

Meanwhile Scottish kings sometimes struggled for power among themselves, as with the MacBeth episode.

MACBETH (b.1005, king 1040-1057). Grandson of Malcolm II, MacBeth was Commander of the army of Duncan I, but had a legitimate claim to the throne of Scotland himself. He killed Duncan in battle in 1040 (not by murder as in Shakespeare's play), and became king. He brought unity, stability and some prosperity to Scotland, making pilgrimages to Rome and ruling wisely until he was himself killed in battle by Malcolm Canmore in 1057.

MALCOLM III (b.1031, king 1058-93). Known as 'Canmore' (which in Gaelic can mean either Great Chief or Big Head), his father, Duncan I, had been killed by MacBeth. Brought up in England in the court of Edward the Confessor, he eventually arrived in Scotland with an army. Helped by the victory of Siward, Earl of Northumbria, over MacBeth in 1054, Malcolm met MacBeth in battle at Lumphanan in 1057 and killed him, afterwards killing MacBeth's family as well.

He established Dunfermline as his capital and, encouraged by his second wife Margaret, he introduced Normans into his court, granting lands and estates to Norman lords in Scotland, but he also carried out Margaret's charitable reforms. Through her infuence, the Lowlands (formerly purely Celtic in culture) became anglicised but, faced with border disputes, Canmore led a series of raids into England. During his fifth raid, Malcolm was killed by an English Norman knight at Alnwick (1093) and is buried at Dunfermline. The shock killed Margaret, who died three days later.

QUEEN MARGARET (c.1046-93). Grand-daughter of England's king Edmund Ironside, her father had fled to Hungary, where she was raised, when Canute seized power in England. Her family returned to England to the court of her great-uncle, Edward the Confessor, in 1057. When he died, Margaret came to Scotland and, in 1069, married the widowed Malcolm Canmore at Dunfermline. She brought with her the 'Holy Rood', a sacred relic supposed to contain a fraction of Christ's cross.

Queen Margaret was devout, and tried to bring the Scottish Church into line with Roman Catholic orthodoxy, taking advice from the Archbishop of Canterbury and founding a Benedictine priory at Dunfermline in 1070. She encouraged Norman clerics to the court and advised her husband Malcolm on charitable social, economic and educational reforms. After her death, she was canonised, becoming SAINT Margaret, and is buried at Dunfermline Abbey. St Margaret's Chapel in Edinburgh Castle, dedicated to her, is believed to date from the reign of David I.

DAVID I (b.1084, king 1124-53). Youngest son of Malcolm Canmore and Margaret, succeeded his brother Alexander I as king in 1124. Like his father, David was brought up in England and invited Anglo-Normans to Scotland. Communal Celtic laws were replaced by feudalism (broadly, that the king owned all the land, granting estates to barons in return for their allegiance). But David's reign marked the beginning of a 'Golden Age' in Scotland: trading with the Continent opened up and coinage was minted. Most notably, David is remembered as a pious builder of religious centres, such as the great Abbeys of Melrose, Newbattle and Dunfermline (where he is buried). As a reward, the Pope granted that the Scottish Church be directly responsible to Rome rather than through Canterbury.

DUNFERMLINE ABBEY

ST. MARGARET'S CHAPEL

EDINBURGH CASTLE

In 1286, King Alexander III was killed in a riding accident. Next in line to the throne was his granddaughter, 3-year-old princess **Margaret of Norway**. England's **Edward I** (1239-1307), known as 'Hammer of the Scots', had plans to subdue Scotland and quickly expoited the situation, offering his son as husband to Margaret. The Guardians of Scotland, knowing the risks, agreed under the conditions of the Treaty of Birgham (1290) which were, in essence:

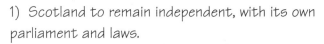

EDWARD I

1) Scotland to remain independent, with its own parliament and laws.
2) No Scot to do homage to the king of England.
3) No English military bases or garrisoned castles on Scottish soil.

Crossing the North Sea from Norway, little Margaret tragically died on the voyage at Orkney, possibly of seasickness. There were now 15 claimants to the vacant throne, so the Guardians asked Edward to arbitrate. The scheming Edward selected **John Balliol** who, though he had the best claim to the Scottish throne, was someone he could control as puppet king. Balliol, known in Scotland as 'Toom Tabbard' ('Empty Coat') had to pay

homage to Edward and accept his own subordinate role, attending Edward's court and having to raise money to pay for Edward's wars. Eventually even Balliol refused Edward's demands and formed an alliance with France, the English king's chief enemy. Balliol eventually fled into exile, abandoning his superficial title.

Edward planned to capture and assimilate the whole of Scotland, making it part of England, and now saw his opportunity to use more violent means. He sent his invasion forces into Scotland to loot, burn, plunder and occupy. Determined to remove any symbol of Scottish nationhood, he had his troops steal the 'Stone of Destiny',

a stone seat used in Scotland's coronation ceremonies, and had it placed under the English throne in Westminster Abbey.

The stone remained there until 1996, when Prime Minister John Major, hoping desperately (and failing miserably) to win Scottish votes in the approaching general election, had it returned to Scotland.

Rather than humiliate the Scots as was his intention, Edward, ironically, did more to strengthen Scottish national awareness and to help shape Scottish identity, because a popular uprising, led by **WILLIAM WALLACE** (1270-1305), erupted against Edward's occupying forces.

LLIAM WALLACE

Wallace, born at Elderslie, was the second son of Sir Malcolm Wallace (who had refused to pay homage to Edward), chief vassal of the Steward of Scotland . At the age of 26, William Wallace killed the Sheriff of Lanark and started the uprising.

Conducting guerrilla warfare from the forests, he led unexpected raids, hiding and moving on after each attack. Castles and garrisons fell to the Scottish resistance. Wallace showed that the English army was not invincible. To the north, Andrew de Moray, the Scottish uprising's other leader, seized the castles of Inverness, Aberdeen, Forfar, Montrose and others, joining forces with Wallace.

At the hour-long **Battle of Stirling Bridge** (1297), the people of Scotland defeated Edward's army the first major battle of the Wars of Independence. The Earl of Surre commanding the English army, fled and the garrison of Stirling Castle surrendered.

The Wars of Independence are a period of Scottish history inspiring some Scots to swell with rampant patriotism, others to cringe with embarrassment, and yet others to make jokes during Scotland-England World Cup football matches. But if they hadn't occurred, Scotland would not now have any claim to self-government or a Scottish parliament.

Unlike most mediaeval warfare, the uprising was not merely a struggle between aristocracy and aristocracy for land and power. Wallace's army was essentially a popular army comprised of common people, with little help from the Scottish nobility, who were torn between loyalty and self-interest.

Nor should it be seen as a racial or tribal conflict between Scots and English. Quite simply, the people of Scotland, whatever their descent - Gaelic, Briton or Anglian - did not want to be ruled from outside, particularly by a state which wanted to destroy their culture and identity and enforce its own upon them through harsh laws and military occupation. And Edward I was not the kind of man who would be moved by a peaceful demonstration or a major leaflet campaign!

Wallace was elected Guardian of Scotland, restoring Scots to positions of authority and writing to trading towns on the Continent that normal Scottish-European trading links could now be resumed.

But Edward began to fight back fiercely, with siege engines, Greek fire and fresh armies. At the **Battle of Falkirk** (1298), Wallace's army was defeated, he gave up his position as Guardian and his campaign began to fail until 1305 when Wallace, betrayed by a Scottish knight and vassal to Edward, Sir John Menteith, was hunted down, captured and tried for treason at Westminster. Wallace protested: 'I am not a traitor to Edward as Edward is not my king!'.

Wallace was hung, drawn, emasculated and quartered, and his severed body parts were stuck on spikes over the towns of Newcastle, Berwick-upon-Tweed, Perth and, reportedly, Aberdeen (though Stirling is more probable) as a public warning against any further Scottish rebellion.

ROBERT THE BRUCE

Public feeling ran higher than ever, however, so now the Scottish nobility, seeing their opportunity, took charge. **ROBERT THE BRUCE** (1274-1329), Earl of Carrick and claimant to the Scottish throne, became King of Scots in 1306, assuming leadership of the struggle. He was

crowned at Scone Abbey by Isabella, Countess of Buchan. Robert the Bruce had actually served on the side of Edward, even holding the offices of Governor of Carlisle and Sheriff of Lanark, but was secretly in league with the Bishop of St Andrews and others hostile to Edward, waiting for the appropriate moment to claim the throne of Scotland. He killed his rival claimant to the throne, John Comyn, in a quarrel in a church at Dumfries, and was later crowned and led battles against Edward's army. Today his body is buried under the pulpit of Dunfermline Abbey church (except for his heart, which is buried in a lead casket at Melrose Abbey - or rather, reburied, since the casket was opened for scientific investigation in 1997).

When Edward 1 died in 1307, he was immediately succeeded by his foppish, less competent son, **Edward II**. Bruce's campaign to reclaim Scotland now became somewhat easier so that, by 1314, only Stirling, Bothwell and Berwick Castles

remained under occupation by English forces. Edward II sent a relief expedition to confront the Scots. Until this date, Bruce's kingship was probationary (or so Barrow, Bruce's most eminent biographer, indicates). This was soon to change.

On 23 June 1314, the two sides met at the **BATTLE OF BANNOCKBURN**, near Stirling: the ultimately decisive battle of the war.

On the Scottish side, Highlanders as well as Lowlanders, Anglo-Scots as well as Celts, all turned out, united in a common struggle. At a crucial moment, it was once again the peasants and common people who saved the day. Towards the end of the battle (by which time the Scots were winning anyway), extra numbers of peasants armed with spears ('Small Folk', as they were called) appeared from over the high ground. Edward's routed army, seeing more reinforcements, made a hasty retreat, fleeing homeward.

To this day, some Scots have the date '1314' tattooed on their bodies, while others feel apologetic, as if Bannockburn had been some kind of anti-English atrocity. But if the battle had gone the other way, ending in a Scottish defeat, Scotland by today may well have become merely an English county (as happened with Cornwall, for example), with no legal or constitutional right to anything more than a regional council, let alone a national parliament with legislative powers.

A declaration of independence - the **DECLARATION OF ARBROATH** - was afterwards drawn up and signed by Scotland's barons in 1320, for submission to and acceptance by the Pope. To paraphrase, it generally states that:

We have chosen our Prince, Robert, to be our sovereign king...but should he give up what we have begun and agree to make our kingdom subject to the English, we shall exert ourselves at once to drive him out and choose another king...

(This shows an early, if limited, form of democracy, comparable with England's Magna Carta, subjecting the power of the king to that of his followers.)

For so long as a hundred of us remain alive we shall never submit ourselves, under any circumstances, to the domination of English rule...
For it is not honour, nor riches, nor glory that we fight and contend for, but for liberty alone.

So that, then, is how Scotland, as a nation-state, came to be formed. It remains a nation in the eyes of its people to this day, though not a state, as it has since become absorbed into Great Britain.

How did this happen? To cut a long story short, economics, religion and the question of the monarchy combined to move Scotland's ruling classes to consider union with England as a way of securing peace. Let's go into this in more detail.

towards the union with england

Scotland's independence was settled and recognised by the **Treaty of Northampton** in 1328, but England often attempted to seize the fertile, productive border counties. Edward III of England did indeed occupy them for a while, after overwhelmingly defeating a Scottish army at the **Battle of Halidon Hill** (1333), a disastrous battle for the Scots, but he gave up after finding them too costly to defend and maintain. During a raid on Dunbar Castle by the Earl of Salisbury in 1338, 'Black Agnes', **Countess of Dunbar**, held off the English forces. When the catapult stones harmlessly struck the solid castle walls, she taunted the enemy by ordering a maid to wipe the dust off the ramparts with a napkin!

ES THE SPIRITED, NTESS OF DUNBAR

I CAN WIPE M AWAY WITH A DUSTER!

England was becoming one of Europe's leading powers, with France as its main rival. To protect itself, Scotland secured an alliance with France. This did not help its relationship with England, which now saw Scotland no longer merely as a nuisance but as a potential power base for England's main enemy.

The rivalry between England and France had begun as far back as the 12th century. After the Norman conquest of England (1066), the Norman English kings ruled much of France as well as England. But between 1180-1223 and 1223-1226 the French kings Philip Augustus and Louis VIII (respectively) acquired the French territories except for Gascony. This area remained fought over until finally won by France from England's Edward III at the end of the so-called Hundred Years War (1337-1453).

When the last of the Bruce line of Scottish kings (**David II**) died in 1371, David's cousin Robert was approved by the Estates (as the Scottish Parliament was called) as king, becoming **Robert II** (b. 1316 king 1371-90). He was the son of Walter, High Steward of Scotland, and so began the **STUART** (or Stewart) line of the monarchy.

But Robert was a mediocre man who couldn't ride a horse, and neither he nor his successor **Robert III** (b. 1340, king 1390-1406) could control Scotland very well. In the borders, baron fought baron and, in the Highlands, clan chief fought clan chief. In fact, Robert III's brother **Robert, Duke of Albany**, largely controlled the government of Scotland.

The Middle Ages lasted from the end of the Dark Ages in the 10th century until the beginning of the Renaissance in the 15th. The Renaissance ('rebirth' of Europe) which followed as a result of relative peace, saw a resurgence of intellectual achievement. Universities flourished. Science, art and literature prospered. Printing was introduced, the Americas discovered and sea routes to the East explored.

Renaissance

At this point, let's take a look at the continuous line of Stuart kings: the Jameses.

JAMES I (b. 1394, king 1406-1437): Attempted to make the Scottish aristocracy submit to royal authority. Formed a close alliance with France (his eldest daughter married the Dauphin). Assassinated by a group of nobles led by the Earl of Atholl. Commissioned the Great Hall at Linlithgow Palace (which would become the birthplace of Mary Queen of Scots).

JAMES II (b. 1430, king 1437-1460): As England had renerwed its claims to Scotland, he attacked English outposts in Scotland and was killed during the **siege of Roxburgh Castle**. Acquired Mons Meg, the enormous siege cannon at Edinburgh Castle, the most impressive artillery weapon in Europe at that time.

JAMES III (b. 1452, king 1460-1488): He established Edinburgh as the official capital. His reign was, however, weakened by a series of rebellions by powerful nobles. He was captured after his defeat at the **Battle of Sauchieburn** and killed by one of the rebels.

JAMES IV

JAMES IV (b. 1473, king 1488-1513): Invaded England on behalf of Perkin Warbeck, a claimant to the English throne, in 1495, but concluded a treaty with King Henry VII in 1502 and married his daughter, Margaret. Commissioned the 'Great Michael' warship - twice the size of England's 'Mary Rose'. When Henry VIII invaded France in 1513, James invaded England where he was killed at the disastrous **Battle of Flodden**.

JAMES V (b. 1512, king 1513-1542): Upheld Catholicism against the Protestant nobles. He signed a treaty with Henry VIII in 1534, but married Marie de Guise, a French noblewoman and allied with France against England. He was defeated by Henry's invading forces at **Solway Moss** in 1542 and died three weeks later, 6 days after the birth of his daughter, Mary.

JAMES V

LANDMARKS OF THE
SCOTTISH
RENAISSANCE

THE 'GREAT MICHAEL'

ST LEONARD'S COLLEGE 1512

PRINTING PRESS INTRODUCED, 1507

ST. ANDREWS UNIVERSITY 1412

ABERDEEN UNIVERSITY 1495

MONS MEG

ROYAL COLLEGE OF SURGEONS 1505

"ANE SATIRE OF THE THREE ESTATES" BY SIR DAVID LYNDESAY

A POLITICAL SATIRE PLAY, LAMPOONING THE CHURCH. PERFORMED BEFORE JAMES V IN 1540, WHO WAS AMUSED AND IMPRESSED!

FALKLAND PALACE

41

It was inevitable that England, being larger and stronger, would draw the smaller country, Scotland, into its influence, but there were factors other than military strength involved.

Religion, for example, played a part as the Protestant Reformation helped pave the way for the Union of Crowns and later the Union of Parliaments. Like that of many other European countries, Scotland's history becomes tied up with religion at this point. Bigotry and religious civil war would stain Scottish history for a long time.

SO WHAT'S THIS "PROTESTANT REFORMATION", THEN?

By the end of the Middle Ages, many in the Catholic Church saw it as having become corrupted by earthly wealth and power, or disagreed with some of its teachings, but criticism and dissent were not permitted. Any clergy who publicly disagreed with the authority of the Pope risked trial for heresy and could face torture, execution or imprisonment. Those who hoped to reform the Church from within were sought out and arrested. At last the reformers saw no alternative but to split from the Pope and set up

denominations of the Reformed (Protestant) Church outside, usually under the protection of northern European princes, who often used the new faith for their own personal motives.

One such prince was England's king, **Henry VIII** (1491-1547, king from 1509), who turned away from Rome to form the Church of England after the Pope refused to grant him a divorce.

During a war with France, of which Scotland was still an ally, Henry's army defeated the Scots at the Battle of Flodden (1513), a costly battle to Scotland, which ensured English superior military status from then on. In 1544 Henry sent troops into Scotland, plundering and burning towns. Four border abbeys were destroyed, the Palace of Holyrood looted and part of Edinburgh burned.

But Scotland itself was undergoing change. Led by the preacher **JOHN KNOX**, the Church of Scotland broke ties with Rome, becoming a Protestant denomination. Hardly surprising, really. Anti-clericalism was becoming widespread and the clergy itself was often lax, ignoring celibacy rules. By the 16th century, 20% of 'legitimization' of bastards was for the clergy's illegitimate children.

John Knox (1512 or 1513-1572) was ordained as a Catholic priest in 1536 but, after the burning at the stake of the reformer George Wishart outside St Andrews castle on the orders of Cardinal Beaton, Archbishop of St Andrews, he became a zealous Protestant, stirring up popular support and leading the Reformation in Scotland. He served two years as a galley slave as punishment for his activities, but this only made him stronger. In Geneva in the mid 1550s he came under the influence of the fanatical Protestant **John Calvin** (1509-1564). Calvin's hellfire-and-brimstone fundamentalism taught that only a chosen few are favoured by God and that everyone else is condemned to damnation. While this is rarely accepted today, Knox's idea of church organisation - Presbyterianism - would come to be accepted by the Church of Scotland in the 1580s. The Scottish Church (the 'Kirk', as it is commonly known) remains Presbyterian today, that is, governed by 'elders', lay members elected from below. The Church of England, by contrast, is an Episcopalian church, governed by bishops appointed from above. But both are Protestant.

The Reformation helped change Scottish society, allowing some intellectual freedom, but many beautiful abbeys, monasteries, cathedrals and churches were destroyed by angry Protestant mobs or troops, and Scotland's Catholic Queen Mary was exiled and was executed by the English authorities.

Mary Stuart, **'MARY QUEEN OF SCOTS'** (1542-1587) became queen in her first year of life on the death of her father, James V. Brought up in France, she married the dauphin (heir to the French throne), later Francis II of France. Francis died in 1560 and Mary returned to Scotland the following year, but by now Scotland had become Protestant and Mary was Catholic (though she allowed religious freedom and toleration). She married her cousin Henry Stuart, **Lord Darnley**, and by him bore a son, James (later James VI of Scotland and I of England), but the couple quarrelled a lot, Darnley being an arrogant and irresponsible playboy. Darnley assisted in the murder of Mary's secretary **Davide Rizzio** (suspecting him of being the father of the child, for which there is no evidence whatsoever), but was himself murdered in 1567 in a plot possibly organised by the **Earl of Bothwell**, whom Mary later married.

MARY QUEEN OF SCOTS

Rebellion followed; Mary was forced to abdicate and was imprisoned at Loch Leven Castle. In 1568 she was rescued by daring teenager Willie Douglas, and escaped to raise an army, but was defeated at the Battle of Langside, near Glasgow, that same year. She fled to England, seeking political asylum from her cousin, Elizabeth I, but Elizabeth saw her as a potential threat to the English (Protestant) monarchy. Indeed, many English Catholic nobles believed Mary to be the rightful queen of England. Elizabeth imprisoned her but Catholics plotted to place Mary on the English throne.

ELIZABETH I

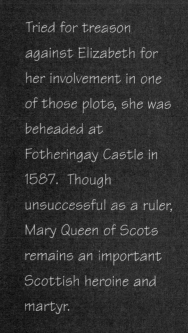

Tried for treason against Elizabeth for her involvement in one of those plots, she was beheaded at Fotheringay Castle in 1587. Though unsuccessful as a ruler, Mary Queen of Scots remains an important Scottish heroine and martyr.

But perhaps the most significant impact of the Reformation in Scotland was that it appealed to the up-and-coming bourgeoisie, the business-owning class, who were starting to replace the landowning aristocracy as the holders of wealth and power. For by now commercial trading was becoming more profitable than the traditional source of wealth - agriculture - and this would continue in the future through European colonisation of the Americas. The Protestant ethic of hard work and reward appealed to the bourgeoisie's sense of enterprise and competition. It would greatly influence Scottish society for a long time to come.

God helps those who help themselves
→
KNOX

FOR A CENTURY NOW, WE MERCHANTS AND TRADERS HAVE FORMED THE 'THIRD ESTATE' OF THE SCOTTISH PARLIAMENT, BUT THE TITLED NOBILITY ARE STILL IN CONTRO

IT'S ALL GOT TO CHANGE. EVEN THE HUMBLEST-BORN SHOULD BE ABLE TO CONTROL THE GOVERNMENT. AS LONG AS THEY'VE BECOME **RICH**, OF COURSE.

HMPH!

Queen Mary's Protestant son James (1566-1625) became **KING JAMES VI** of Scotland in 1567 - and was to become JAMES I of England. Under his reign, much religious intolerance and persecution followed. James believed in the 'Divine Right of Kings', i.e. that the king rules with the authority of God and therefore no-one has the right to question the king's authority. James was anti-Catholic and his nobles played on this. His alleged homosexual relationship with his French cousin Esme Stewart, Duke of Lennox, ended when James' nobles accused Lennox of being a Catholic spy and persuaded James to stop protecting him. Esme was recalled to France and James clamped down even further on Catholicism.

49

But James' wrath was turned most savagely towards those accused of witchcraft. In his book *Daemonologie* (1597), he imagined the Devil's agents everywhere. Perhaps he reasoned that, if treason against the king is the work of the Devil, then what better way to turn people off treason than to stir up popular fear of the Devil in everyday life? Witchcraft persecutions in Scotland would continue throughout James' reign and afterwards (such as in the 1640s, under the Covenanters). Some estimates (Geddes & Grosset, 1997) claim 1,350 alleged witches in Scotland were killed - almost 3 times as many as in England. Nearly half of those tried were burned at the stake, about 80% of them women.

WHERE'S THAT DEVIL ?

LONDON, 1603

ALAS! OUR QUEEN, ELIZABETH, IS DEAD, LEAVING NO HEIR. WHO WILL BE OUR NEXT KING OR QUEEN? (REMEMBER, THEY MUST BE PROTESTANT).

HER NEXT OF KIN IS HER COUSIN, KING JAMES VI OF SCOTLAND. UNLIKE HIS MOTHER, MARY STUART, HE WAS RAISED IN THE PROTESTANT FAITH. HE CAN BE KING OF ENGLAND AND SCOTLAND.

55

James' cousin Queen Elizabeth I of England died, leaving no heir. As he was her next of kin, the English offered him the throne of England. He gladly accepted and the **UNION OF CROWNS** (1603) meant that Scotland and England would share the same crown. For the time being, they still had separate parliaments but, as James moved his court to London, and Parliament's duty was to carry out Crown authority, Scotland was effectively ruled from London, losing it's diplomatic power. James himself hoped Scotland would eventually become absorbed like an English county, or 'with time become as Cumberland and Northumberland and those other remote and distant shires'.

James' son, **Charles I** (1600-1649, king from 1625), tried to absorb the Scottish Church into the Anglican (Church of England) tradition. He was resisted by the Scottish **COVENANTERS**, who signed a declaration called the **National Covenant** on 28 February 1638, swearing to defend their right to uphold their own form of worship, and to oppose the imposition and interference of the king. Royalists would come to see this as treason.

CHARLES I

THE COVENANT WAS CREATED BY REV. ALEXANDER HENDERSON, A KIRK MINISTER, AND JOHNSTON OF WARISTON, A LAWYER.

FIRST TO SIGN WAS THE 5TH EARL OF MONTROSE.

OVER 150 NOBLES SIGNED THE ORIGINAL DECLARATION.

WHAT ABOUT WOMEN?

The introduction of Anglican bishops and prayer books was much disliked. A later 19th-century tale alleges that **Jenny Geddes** (c.1600-1660), a street vegetable seller in Edinburgh, actually threw her stool at the Dean of St Giles Cathedral, narrowly missing his head.

JENNY GEDDES

In England, Civil War (1642-1649) broke out between the pro-monarchist 'Cavaliers', who supported the king's authority, and the pro-Parliament 'Roundheads', led by **Oliver Cromwell**, who sought to abolish the monarchy and establish the 'Commonwealth', a republic with an elected parliament.

CROMWELL

In 1643 the Covenanters joined with the English Parliamentarians in signing the **Solemn League and Covenant**, promising military aid to the Roundheads in return for the establishment of Presbyterianism in England. Charles surrendered to a Scottish army at Newark in 1646, which then handed him over to the English.

After the defeat of the Royalists, Charles I was beheaded. Following the king's death, the Covenanters sought to return his exiled son **Charles II** as monarch, provided he upheld the rights of the Covenant, but they were defeated by Cromwell at Dunbar (1650). Three years later, Cromwell forcibly united Scotland and England under a single parliament in London. Scotland was occupied by English armies, was taxed more heavily than under the monarchy, and grew poorer while England grew stronger and richer. By the time of Cromwell's death in 1658, the Scots wanted to bring back the monarchy.

In England, too, they had had enough. Parliament, purged of Royalists and moderates, was dissolved by Cromwell, who became 'Lord Protector', taking absolute control of Great Britain in order to 'safeguard its interests'. With the death of Cromwell, England's leaders also sought a restoration of the monarchy, though Cromwell's son Richard became Protector until the Restoration.

The Restoration in 1660, putting Charles II on the throne, ended Cromwell's brief, unwelcome union which had lasted only 8 years, and gave Scotland back its independent Edinburgh Parliament (under the Crown in London of course, as before). But from now on, Parliament would make laws. The Crown, in time, would merely make them official. However Parliament, though no longer the preserve of the landed aristocracy, was elected only by people earning over a certain (very large) income: the common people were not yet allowed to vote.

Charles was Episcopalian and never set foot in Scotland, where religious sectarian fighting continued. When Charles, like his father, tried again to introduce Episcopalian influences into the Kirk, some extreme Covenanters again hoped to see Presbyterianism in England as well as Scotland.

John Maitland, Duke of Lauderdale (from 1672), had formerly been a zealous Covenanter, but had switched sides, joining the Royalists in 1647. Created High Commissioner for Scotland 1667-1679, he came up from London (he was himself Scottish) with the task of looking after Scotland on behalf of the king, bringing the Scottish Church to order and putting down dissent. Persecution of Covenanters continued after his term of office, and the 1680s are known as the 'Killing Time'.

THERE WE GO. ONE MONARCHY RESTORED.

PLOP

CHARLES II

NOW, ABOUT THE REINTRODUCTION OF BISHOPS...

GRRR

NO' AGAIN!

PRAYER BOOK

JINGS, THAT MAKES ME MAD

58

While the Covenanter men fought battles, wrote declarations and preached on moors or hillsides at risk of life, the women gave active support and suffered accordingly. **Mary Howie** of Auchinleck, Ayrshire, was ordered by Royalist troops to take an oath abjuring Covenanting principles. When she refused, the soldiers burned her fingers over a fire until the bones were bare and black - a form of torture used frequently.

When Royalist soldiers charged upon a Covenanter hill meeting near Cumnock, **Marion Cameron** (sister of a leading Covenanter, Richard Cameron) and two others hid among the moss near the village of Dalgig. Thinking themselves safe, they began to sing hymns. But the soldiers heard and found them, ordering them to burn their bibles or die. When the women refused, they were shot on the spot.

Many other women were similarly attacked, or were raped, exiled, or branded on the cheek, while yet more died through cold or illness contracted while hiding in caves or on moors.

When Charles died he was succeeded as king by his brother, **James VII** (II of England). James was Catholic and began to reassert Catholicism into both his kingdoms. The last straw came when he had a son, James Edward Stuart. This meant the continuation of a Catholic monarchy. The Protestant ruling classes feared the eventual reintroduction of the 'Power of Rome' and therefore decided to change the royal dynasty. In 1688 they deposed James, who fled into exile in France, and replaced him with the Protestant prince **William of Orange** (a Dutch province), husband of James' daughter **Mary**, crowning him in London as William III (II of Scotland). This change of dynasty became known as the 'Glorious Revolution' in England because it happened without bloodshed. In Scotland, however, armed conflict continued between those who supported William and those loyal to James - JACOBITES (from the Latin name for James, Jacobus).

WILLIAM III

Jacobites were not necessarily Catholic. **John Graham of Claverhouse** (Viscount 'Bonnie' Dundee), a Protestant, led a revolt of Highlanders against William immediately. They won a victory at the **Battle of Killiecrankie** (July 1689), but Dundee was killed by a stray bullet and his army was defeated a month later at Dunkeld by the Cameronians, a newly-formed Scottish regiment.

James himself raised a Jacobite army in Ireland, but was defeated there by William at the Battle of the Boyne (1690).

I'LL CRUSH THESE JACOBITES OR I'M A DUTCHMAN!

WILLIAM III

As many Jacobites were Highland chiefs William, to exercise control, decreed that all clan chiefs take an Oath of Loyalty to him, giving them until 1 January 1692. On 31 December 1691, the chief of the MacDonalds of Glencoe turned up at Fort William to sign the Oath. But he hadn't moved fast enough for the authorities' liking, and they would make him pay the price in blood: his clan would be used as an example to any Highlanders who might show disloyalty.

BUT YOU ARE, DEAR.

PSST! CAMPBELL!

YOUR CLAN AND TH MACDONALDS ARE O ENEMIES, AREN'T YO I MIGHT HAVE A LITTLE JOB FOR YOU

The Clan Campbell was selected to carry out a macabre secret mission: the act of treachery that is now called the GLENCOE MASSACRE.

Posing as peaceful visitors, the Campbells were welcomed by the MacDonalds into their homes where, on the night of 12 February 1692, they murdered their hosts as they lay in bed. Those MacDonalds who escaped and fled to the hills met rifle fire from waiting troops, or starvation and exposure in the hills.

The Campbells had been ordered 'for the good of the country' to 'put to the sword all under 70'. In Scotland, it was regarded as a heinous act of 'murder under trust'.

NEVER MIND. WE CAN ALWAYS EMIGRATE.

* "LOOK O

* GARDYLOO:

Scotland remained very poor, the land bearing little wealth. One in six Scots was a beggar, and famine as well as unemployment was rife. The tenements of Edinburgh were dirty and overcrowded and even the houses of the professional classes were cramped. To escape this, the poor could choose emigration while the wealthy could turn to investment in trade. Scottish emigrants settled in English colonies in America such as New Jersey and, in 1684, a party of Presbyterian settlers arrived at Stuart's Town in South Carolina, but were nearly destroyed within a year by Spanish attacks from Florida. Scotland needed a trading colony of its own. England was prospering from its colonies in North America so, hoping to follow suit and bring money into Scotland, it was decided to establish a Scottish colony at Darien, Panama, in 1698. It was to be called 'New Caledonia' (not to be confused with today's New Caledonia in French Polynesia in the Pacific).

ANY SPARE CHANGE, PAL?

AH WIS GAUNNY AS. YOU!

The idea of forming a Scottish colony was first discussed in 1681 by the Scottish Privy Council. The Scottish Parliament passed an Act 12 years later to encourage foreign trade. In 1695 the Scottish Africa and India company was formed by **William Paterson,** the Scot who founded the Bank of England. The directors hoped to raise funds from English investors, but these

NEW ENGLAND

were dissuaded when the East India Company in London persuaded the English Parliament to stop them. The Scottish directors then 'went public', turning to the Scottish people and raising £400,000 from public subscription, at that time equivalent to nearly all the Scottish coin in circulation.

THESE MOSQUITOS ARE WORSE THAN THE MIDGES.

NEW CALEDONIA

But in Panama the Scottish colonists found to their dismay a mosquito-infested swamp. Those who survived malaria and yellow fever were harrassed by Spanish troops. When they asked the English colonies for help, King William refused, not wishing to make enemies of the Spanish, who might then form an alliance with France (still England's main enemy and rival, competing for overseas expansion). So the Darien colony was a complete disaster. But even if it had been successful, it is doubtful whether England would have allowed it to continue. Even though Scotland and England shared the same king, the English ruling class of the day would not have easily tolerated a rival on its own doorstep.

The Scottish ruling class now saw only one way to save Scotland: a Union of Parliaments with England, forming Great Britain.

The idea of a Union of Parliaments was actually first proposed by the monarchy. Back in 1603, James VI & I, addressing his English Parliament, had said:

I AM THE HUSBAND AND THE WHOLE ISLE IS MY LAWFUL WIFE. I HOPE THEREFORE NO MAN WILL BE SO UNREASONABLE AS TO THINK THAT I, THAT AM A CHRISTIAN KING UNDER THE GOSPEL, SHOULD BE A POLYGAMIST AND THE HUSBAND OF TWO WIVES.

In 1702 King William, worrying about a possible return of Jacobitism, urgently appealed from his deathbed to the English Parliament, stating that:

NOTHING CAN CONTRIBUTE MORE TO THE PRESENT AND FUTURE PEACE, SECURITY AND HAPPINESS OF ENGLAND AND SCOTLAND THAN A FIRM AND ENTIRE UNION.

Later that year his successor, Queen Anne, urged the English Parliament at the beginning of her reign...

TO CONSIDER OF PROPER METHODS OF ATTAINING A UNION WITH SCOTLAND.

James Douglas, 2nd Duke of Queensberry, persuaded the Scottish Parliament to pass an Act enabling the Queen to appoint commissioners to negotiate a Treaty of Union. The Scottish and English delegations of commissioners first met at Westminster on 10 November 1702. Not well attended, the proceedings were taken up by arguments about trade. The negotiations were postponed until, 3 years later, after bitter trade disputes between the two countries, the question of sending commissioners to Westminster was again raised in the Scottish Parliament.

On 16 April 1706, the two groups of commissioners met at Westminster again. After 2 months of debating, arguing and bargaining, the terms were agreed and laid out in the Treaty of Union. The 25 Articles it contained included:

1) A single UK parliament in Westminster, comprising at that time of 190 English lords, 16 Scottish; 513 English/Welsh commoners, 45 Scottish.
2) A common currency and English weights and measures to be used universally.
3) Armed forces united under a single UK defence system.
4) A single flag for the whole United Kingdom - the crosses of St Andrew and St George together, forming the 'Union Jack'.

"ALL THOSE AGAINST UNION: TOUGH!"

On 12 October 1706 the terms were presented to the Scottish Parliament. As soon as news of the terms leaked out, there was uproar. Crowds in Edinburgh and Glasgow took to the streets chanting 'No Union! No Union!'. In Dumfries, copies of the terms were burned in public. On 8 and 9 November, Glasgow mobs rioted and a national revolt seemed a possibility. The Scottish Parliament banned the carrying of guns, but this only stirred up more violence. The Glasgow crowds broke into the Tolbooth and ransacked houses, looking for weapons. Dragoons were sent to quell the disturbance, arresting ringleaders.

90 petitions against the Union poured in to the Scottish Parliament, from a third of the shires, a quarter of the Royal Burghs and from local parishes. Despite this, and despite a proposal from the **Duke of Atholl** to hold an election on the matter, the petitions were ignored. When bribery started to be used to move Scots MPs to vote for Union, the **Duke of Hamilton** planned to raise 7000 men to storm the Parliament. He abandoned the idea at the last minute, however.

L THOSE IN FAVOUR..."

AYE!

Concessions were offered. Scotland would retain its own law and education systems and its own Church. Nevertheless, it was described by anti-Union MP Lord Belhaven as 'entire surrender'. Another, Andrew Fletcher of Saltoun, called for trading links - an economic treaty - while remaining independent.

But, on 16 January 1707, the Scottish Parliament voted overwhelmingly in favour of the Articles of Union (110 in favour; 69 against). The English Parliament passed the Act on 6 March and **1 MAY 1707 became officially the First day of UNION**. The first British Parliament met on 23 October.

Unlike the Welsh and Irish, who were physically conquered, the Scottish

> BECOMING THE GREATEST BALLY NATION ON EARTH, GOD BLESS US!

Parliament simply sold out. Through self-interest, even succumbing to outright bribery, enough Scots MPs were persuaded to support the Articles of Union. From this point on, while the whole of Britain would be all too often referred to as 'England' by people throughout the world, Scotland has had to fight to keep its identity.

'Ah well! There's an end of an auld sang!' said anti-Union MP James Ogilvie, Earl of Seafield, when the Act of Union vote was passed. But not quite, for Scotland's identity was to survive, at least among her own people, and the struggle to win back self-rule was yet to begin.

Anyway, that is how the Scottish and English states merged, forming the Britain we know. Scotland became (and remains) a nation within a state. Before the Union, Scotland's relationship with England had been defensive. Now what? Would the Union be a partnership of equals? Would the marriage work? Let's see...

Well, not exactly. It was hardly an equal partnership. With such a small number of MPs in a large UK Parliament it was inevitable that Scotland's role would be subservient (even in the 20th century, following the 19th century Reform Acts, Scots had 72 MPs in a UK Parliament of 650, reflecting relative population sizes). From the moment of Union, the Scots became a minority, and decisions affecting Scotland would be made in London. And in many ways the rough end of the deal would be felt most strongly in the Highlands, which had its own culture, language and society separate from Lowland Scotland.

HONI SOIT QUI MAL Y PENSE

While Lowlanders spoke English or Scots (a Scottish derivative of English) and lived like other Europeans as farmers, merchants or urban professionals, the Highland people lived under an ancient feudal clan system, where each clan (a tribe of related families) wore their own distinctive tartan and held their own territory, for which they often fought each other. Living conditions in the Highlands were Iron Age, except for those of the aristocratic chiefs. The Highlanders' language was mostly Gaelic and their religion at that time mainly Catholic or Episcopalian; only later did they convert to the Presbyterianism of the Lowlands. Most significantly, many of their chiefs were Jacobites, supporting the Stuart pretenders to the British throne.

WHAT'S A 'PRETENDER'?

A CLAIMANT T[...] THE POSITION O[...] MONARCH, WHO [...] NOT OFFICIALL[...] RECOGNISED AS SUCH.

OH, RIGHT.

74

James II & VII, you will remember, was deposed. The Jacobites had supported him and continued to support his descendants. There was Jacobite support in England as well as Scotland, but it was particularly strong in the Highlands.

WHY?

SOME - CATHOLICS AND EPISCOPALIANS - FOR RELIGIOUS REASONS, HOPING TO RESTORE A CATHOLIC MONARCHY. BUT LARGELY IT WAS FOR FEUDAL REASONS: AN EXCUSE TO 'HAVE A GO' AT RIVAL CLANS, WHO HAPPENED TO BE ON THE GOVERNMENT SIDE. OTHERS SAW AN OPPORTUNITY TO LOOT AND PLUNDER.

THIS IS FOR GLENCOE, CAMPBELL DOG!

The first great Jacobite Rebellion (1715) was led by **John Erskine**, 11th Earl of Mar, supporter of James III & VIII (known as the 'Old Pretender', as distinct from the 'Young Pretender' - his son, Bonnie Prince Charlie. We'll get to him shortly). After being rebuked by George I, Mar had switched loyalties with such haste that he became known as 'Bobbing John'.

EARL OF MAR

BRING BACK THE STUART MONARCHY!

JACOBITES

At his castle at Braemar, Aberdeenshire, Mar organised a meeting on 27 August 1715 to plan an armed rebellion. On 6 September, the standard of James was raised there and, with his two main commanders, the Earl of Huntly and George Keith, Earl Marischal, Mar led his army southwards, drawing support mainly from the North East.

They seized Perth on 14 September, establishing the town as Mar's headquarters. Mar sent Brigadier William Mackintosh of Bolum south to join up with Dumfriesshire and Northumberland Jacobite forces and then, from the south, attack the Duke of Argyll's government forces at Stirling. After a failed attempt to occupy Edinburgh, Borum joined up with the southern units but Thomas Forster, leader of the Northumbrian force, wanted to push southward through England, counting on support in Lancashire. He was defeated at Preston, Lancashire, on 14 November. Meanwhile Mar, at the indecisive **Battle of Sheriffmuir** (13 Nov 1715), did not exactly lose the battle but had certainly lost the war.

James III landed at Peterhead on 22 December only to find that his cause had been lost. He headed back to France on 4 February 1716, joined by Mar and other leaders of his army. He went to Italy and set up his exiled court in Rome.

CHARLES EDWARD STUART

After the Old Pretender's failure to win the position of king, his Italian-born son, **CHARLES EDWARD STUART** - 'Bonnie Prince Charlie' (1720-1788) - attempted in 1745 (at the age of 24) to reclaim the throne for his father in a much more famous and dramatic event: the **'FORTY FIVE' Rebellion**.

Later, 19th-century romantic writers such as Sir Walter Scott and Robert Louis Stevenson would portray Bonnie Prince Charlie as a brave Highland hero: a daring, dashing figure. Not the impression given by portraits from the actual period: that of a young dandy in camp costume. Nevertheless, his sense of mission was visionary and his resolve firm, though he had a stubbornness of nature that would be his downfall. His refusal to listen to good advice and his conviction in his own erroneous decisions made him push his campaign against the odds and led to final defeat. At any rate, in royalist terms he had a legitimate case for his claim to the throne, but was denied it because of his Catholic beliefs.

Strictly speaking, the 'Forty Five' was not a Scottish national uprising, but a British civil war over a dynastic dispute for the throne, with religion a major issue. Nationalism, however, did play a part. Anti-Union sentiment was still strong in Scotland, and Jacobitism played upon this. Campaign literature issued during the 1715 Rebellion spoke of dissolving the Union of Parliaments and restoring Scotland's independence. This policy was retained by the Young Pretender during the 'Forty Five'.

Even so, the Jacobite cause was not exclusively Scottish. There were Jacobite activists in England, Ireland and Wales. Besides, more Scots fought against Charlie than fought for him. But as most of his support came from the Highlands, that is where his campaign began and ended. Not all Highlanders supported Charles Edward (though they would afterwards all be punished, whether they did or not), but over half of all Highland men joined his cause.

Charles Edward Stuart pawned family treasure (the Sobiewski rubies, his mother's dowry) to raise funds and buy arms. Expecting help from the French, he left France for Scotland with 7 followers (4 of them Irish), landing by boat at the island of Eriskay on 23 July 1745. It was the first time he had ever set foot in Scotland.

Meeting up with followers including Donald Cameron of Lochiel and Sir Alexander MacDonald, Charles raised his father's standard at Glenfinnan on 19 August 1745 and waited for his armies to muster. With 2000 clansmen he marched to Perth, occupying the town and setting up headquarters. Others joined him, including Lord George Murray and James Drummond, Duke of Perth, who were made joint Commanders.

On 17 September, the Jacobites seized Edinburgh without resistance. The city's officials fled to Berwick. On capturing Edinburgh, Charles issued a decree abolishing the Act of Union.

In London, a new verse was added to 'God Save the King', referring to General George Wade, government Commander in Scotland during the 1715 Rebellion and now a Field Marshal:

God grant that Marshal Wade
May by thy mighty aid
Victory bring.
May he sedition hush
And like a torrent rush
Rebellious Scots to crush,
God save the King.

The King, incidentally, was George II.

General Sir John Cope, Commander-in-Chief of the British government forces in Scotland, had set off from Stirling Castle with his troops to seek out and confront the Jacobite army. After scouring the North East, he and his men travelled by ship from Dundee to Dunbar. On 21 September the Jacobites, led by Murray and Drummond under cover of mist, launched a surprise attack on Cope's army at the **Battle of Prestonpans**, near Edinburgh. Each side had about 2300 men, but Cope's 'redcoats' were unprepared and the Jacobites won a quick victory. In only ten minutes, Cope's army was routed. Cope was afterwards court-martialled, but acquitted.

After Prestonpans, the Prince's army pressed on into England. A series of easy victories followed. On 15 November they captured Carlisle. By the 25th they had taken Penrith and Lancaster. The next day they took Preston and, three days later, Manchester (from which most of the Prince's 200 English followers came). By 4 December, they had reached Derby. Charles wanted to advance on London, but by now his army was surrounded by those of Wade and the Duke of Cumberland. French help had not arrived and his leaders advised a withdrawal back to Scotland. Two days later, the reluctant retreat began.

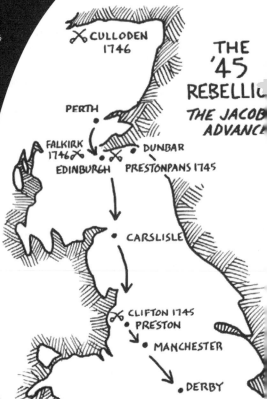

THE '45 REBELLION

THE JACOB ADVANCE

CULLODEN 1746

PERTH

FALKIRK 1746

DUNBAR

EDINBURGH   PRESTONPANS 1745

CARSLISLE

CLIFTON 1745
PRESTON

MANCHESTER

DERBY

LOND

DUKE OF CUMBERLAND?

WILLIAM AUGUSTUS, DUKE OF CUMBERLAND (1721-1765), LATE KNOWN AS 'BUTCHER' CUMBERLAND FOR HIS BRUTAL MISTREATMENT OF HIGHLANDER

Charles' army arrived in Glasgow, where he was not particularly welcome, was treated with complete indifference and found no support. He did, however, find a girlfriend: Clementina Walkinshaw, who later became his mistress in exile.

Moving eastwards, the Jacobites won another major victory over government forces at the second **Battle of Falkirk**, 17 January 1746 (not to be confused with the first one of 1298). The government Commander there, General Henry Hawley, was incompetent, ignoring warnings and afterwards blaming his own men.

But the Jacobite retreat continued northwards into the Highlands before the advance of Cumberland's reinforced army.

THAT'S IT, LADS — I'LL LEAD FROM BEHIND.

The two armies finally clashed at the **BATTLE OF CULLODEN** near Inverness (16 April 1746), *the last military battle in Britain.*

Well outnumbered by Cumberland's better-equipped, well-fed and well-rested men, the tired, hungry Jacobites had little chance. In the slaughter that occurred, 1200 Jacobites died at the hands of the government redcoats (whose casualties numbered 364). With cannon, larger numbers and the use of grapeshot, Cumberland's army won the day.

Afterwards, Cumberland showed no mercy to the wounded and prisoners, killing battlefield survivors. Determined to stamp out any trace of rebel support, his army ravaged the glens, shooting or hanging men, raping women, looting anything of value and burning homes.

With the help of a Highland woman, **FLORA MACDONALD** (1722-1790), who sheltered him and disguised him as her maid, Charles escaped into exile in France, ending up a depressed alcoholic, and the traditional Highland way of life came to an end forever. Flora MacDonald emigrated to America where, rather ironically, she roused and recruited Highland emigrants to fight on the British side in the American War of Independence. She afterwards returned to her native Scotland.

After Culloden, the speaking of the Gaelic language and the civilian wearing of tartan clothing were banned for 10 years, and the Highlands were occupied by a military presence for nearly 100 years.

FLORA MACDONALD

As the 18th century drew to a close, the Highlanders were faced with a much greater tragedy, this time imposed by their own clan chiefs and Highland aristocracy, who were now suddenly very 'British', then later by commercial landowners who bought up the land from the native chiefs: **THE HIGHLAND CLEARANCES**. These waves of human depopulation occurred at different times in different parts of the Highlands on different scales.

THE HIGHLAND CLEARANCES

Like the Lowland aristocracy, the Highland landowners realised that the age of making money from the land was over. The future lay in trade and industry and for the time being that meant textiles. If they were to keep their wealth and status, they had to move with the times and become investors.

Realising that wool production was much more profitable than agriculture, the landowners introduced sheep rearing and evicted the resident crofters or tenant farmers and their families (an area formerly supporting 9 families could be managed by a single shepherd). Families were simply forced out, their homes and crops burned. Resistance was punished with transportation for the ringleaders. The Highlands and Islands were depopulated on a massive scale, thousands of families driven from their lands and forced to migrate to Glasgow and the towns of the Lowlands, or to emigrate in a mass exodus to Canada, America, Australia or New Zealand. The Highlands would have 'modernised' sooner or later, but the brutal methods of the Clearances made it too sudden and painful.

Before the onset of sheep farming, Highlanders were already emigrating, but on a smaller scale. Between 1700 and 1760, fewer than 3000 people emigrated from the Highlands, after which the number increased to c.10,000 between 1760 and 1765.

Other waves of clearances followed, with figures varying. T.M. Devine, an authority on the subject, says that c.10 000 emigrated between 1775 and 1815 ('Clanship to Crofters' War', Manchester, 1994). Tom Steel, author and producer of 'Scotland's Story' (Fontana/Channel 4, 1985) states that 'between 1800 and 1806, nearly 20,000 were evicted from the Highlands and Islands of Scotland'. But then, not all evicted Highlanders emigrated. Many migrated to other parts of Scotland.

In 1852, on the Knoydart peninsula, 400 families were forced out of their homes, which were then demolished. 300 were shipped to Canada, the rest simply made homeless.

Before the Clearances, half of Scotland's population lived in the Highlands. In 1750, the population of Scotland stood at 1,265,000, of which 652,000 were Highlanders. Today Scotland's population is 5 million, and that of the Highlands and Islands only 232,000.

In the 1880s, a new wave of Highland Clearances began, this time to make way for the expansion of deer forest and grouse moor to cater for the hunting and shooting practices of wealthy Victorian tourists. Once again, the landlords (by now very much anglicised and

upper class, with Oxford-Cambridge educations and accents, which distanced them from their tenants) evicted thousands of families, to accommodate their visitors.

"IN IRELAND LANDLORDS HAVE GONE TO THE LENGTH OF SWEEPING AWAY SEVERAL VILLAGES AT ONCE; IN SCOTLAND AREAS AS LARGE AS GERMAN PRINCIPALITIES ARE DEALT WITH... SUFFERINGS HAVE BEEN INFLICTED IN THE HIGHLANDS SCARCELY LESS SEVERE THAN THOSE OCCASIONED BY THE POLICY OF THE NORMAN KINGS".

MARX

THE ONLY EMPLOYMENT TO COME OUT OF THIS WAS OF A SERVILE, SUBSERVIENT, TOADYING NATURE...

GROUSE BEATERS, GHILLIES, GARDENERS, GAMEKEEPERS, DOMESTIC SERVANTS, ETC.

The Highlanders became militant. Inspired by the formation in Ireland of the Irish Land League, Highlanders set up the **Highland Land League** in April 1882 to organise sabotage, squatting and rent strikes. Evictions continued, as did summonses for non-payment of rent, leading to the **'Crofters' War'** (1882-1886), with violent pitched battles between crofters and police. Particularly serious was the **'Battle of the Braes'** near Portree, Skye, in April 1882.

A sheriff officer serving eviction notices to 12 tenants was met by a crowd of 150 crofters, who burned his summonses. 60 police were sent to deal with the crofters. They clashed with a huge crowd of men and women armed with sticks and boulders, who drove the police off.

Agitation spread, and in July 1886, detachments of 750 police and 250 marines were sent to the island of Tiree to keep order, arresting 8 crofters. The following year, 200 crofters invaded the deer estate of Park, Lewis on 22 November, planning to kill the landlord's deer to feed their families and to protest the misuse of land. A gunboat was sent to the area, with 100 troops to stop the incident.

As attempts to bring industry into the Highlands and Islands were not enough to stop the depopulation of the region through unemployment, incidents of squatting by crofters without land (cottars) continued into the 20th century. The Highland Land league campaigned for crofter's rights well into the same century, outbreaks of rural agitation continuing until c.1920.

So, as the Highlands became cleared of their people, the Lowlands became home to most Scots.

Let us turn our attention, then, to the Lowlands...

While the Clearances swept the Highlands in the late 18th Century, Britain's Industrial Revolution was beginning. Even in the Lowlands, small farming and cottage weaving were becoming a less profitable means of income as against large-scale trade and industry.

Poor weavers and evicted farmers, unemployed Lowlanders and dispossessed Highlanders flocked to the factory towns, to the mines and the docks, filling the swelling slums and forming the Scottish working class. The Machine Age had begun.

Living conditions in the town slums were cramped, unsanitary and unhygienic, while working conditions were dangerous and laborious, with long working hours for very low pay. The chattel slavery of past times had been replaced with the 'wage slavery' of the age of industrialisation, whereby people had to work under such conditions merely to live a life the point of which seemed to be to make a profit for the employers. In the villages and the countryside, where life was just as hard and hungry for the poor, traditional handcraft weavers felt their livelihood being taken away from them by growing manufacturing monopolies, unable to compete against the more productive, mechanised industrial methods of factory owners. Everywhere, working people demanded better conditions, to be brought about by political change. When everyone was allowed to vote, it was assumed, they could vote for reform.

95

JOHN PAUL JONES

The radicalism that swept America and the European continent reached Scotland. Many Scots had taken part in the American Revolution and their influence was coming home. America's first navy admiral, **John Paul Jones** (1747-1792), was Scottish-born. After winning a particular sea victory, he declared 'I have not yet begun to fight'. Another Scot, **John Witherspoon**, signed the American Declaration of Independence in 1776. He declared that the time to break away from Britain was 'not only ripe, but rotting'. Of George Washington's 22 brigadier-generals, nine were of Scots descent.

With Scots and English on the American side as well as on the British (and of course Americans on the British side as well as the American), the American War of Independence was therefore a case of civic, not ethnic, nationalism. This is echoed in today's Scotland, where the nationalist movement includes English incomers (as well as black, Asian and other ethnic groups).

Meanwhile, the Scottish Enlightenment had arrived - the period at the end of the 18th century when philosophy became based on reason and individualism rather than tradition. It produced some notable Scottish thinkers, looking at the new science of 'political economy' and how it could affect the way we live. Not all were concerned with social reform. **Adam Smith** (1723-1790) showed how capitalist wealth depends on competition, and rejected the idea of interference in industry by the government or the community.

Edinburgh, 'The Athens of the North', was to be an important meeting place throughout the late 18th and early 19th centuries for great philosophers of the time, including **David Hume** (1711-1776), who taught that knowledge is based on experience (empiricism), and, later, **Thomas Carlyle** (1795-1881), who opposed Adam Smith's views and championed working-class action. Most significantly, the French Revolution (1789-1799) offered encouragement to the labouring poor and the radical literati. People could see that it was possible to rise up against the ruling class and change the style of government.

Edinburgh's educated classes moved from the High Street to the Georgian terraces of the 'New Town', north of Princes Street, planned by James Craig, with their neatly laid out streets, squares and crescents. This would become the focal point of the Scottish Enlightenment.

The political awareness of the 18th century reached the masses. 'Combinations' (forerunners of the trades union), cooperative societies and friendly societies were formed to fight for workers' democratic and employment rights and basic welfare against worsening living and working conditions and rising poverty.

As working people were still denied the right to vote, there were strikes, riots, violent clashes with the authorities and bloodshed at the hands of troops. As elsewhere in Britain, radicalism spread, demanding political change, but with this difference: the labour movement in Scotland included home rule in its demands.

WHY?

Issues like health, education, housing and employment are important to us. We can't necessarily depend on a far-away London government to handle these issues the way we want. Centralisation takes power from the people. Power must be decentralised, so we need a Scottish parliament to exercise democratic control over our own affairs.

So now we arrive at the big issue: the Scottish constitutional question of self-government. For, contrary to popular belief, *the modern movement for self-government began with the labour movement* and not, as is often supposed, only with Celtic patriots. The return of a Scottish parliament was seen as a democratic necessity, along with the right to vote and the right to form trades unions.

1792:

In 1789 French revolutionaries had stormed the Bastille prison in Paris and now, in Edinburgh, rioters burned an effigy of the hated home secretary Henry Dundas (nicknamed in Scotland 'King Harry the Ninth' because his oppressive control was reminiscent of Henry VIII), only to be shot by troops.

Henry Dundas (1742-1811), a lawyer from one of the smaller Scottish aristocratic families, became Tory Home Secretary to Pitt the Younger in 1791, carrying out the prosecution of English as well as Scottish reformers. His grip on the government of Scotland was secure, and such was his power that he had plenty of ambitious, opportunistic followers. Though ruthless with those who fell foul of him, he rewarded loyalty, and those who won his favour could attain positions of power or prestige through his influence. In 1802 he became 1st Viscount Melville, but his corruption and nepotism were eventually found out and, in 1806, he was impeached. Though acquitted (at least of the main charge), he would no longer hold office.

In 1792, the **FRIENDS OF THE PEOPLE** was founded, organising for universal adult suffrage (including women's votes), more frequent general elections and a home rule parliament for Scotland. Mainly led by middle-class intellectuals and professional people, it nevertheless attracted a wide following of working people into its ranks, organising in the towns and villages of the Lowlands.

REV. THOMAS FYSHE PALMER

WILLIAM SKIRVING

THOMAS MUIR

Although the Friends of the People merely sought moderate, democratic reform, the ruling classes of the day saw them as subversive and revolutionary. Sedition was causing anxiety among society's elite. Scottish Jacobitism in its day had been seen as a threat to the existing order. Popular Scottish republicanism was now seen as an even greater threat.

Among the leaders a young lawyer from Glasgow, **THOMAS MUIR**, had contacted a Dublin-based political reform (later republican nationalist) group called the United Irishmen, led by Theobald Wolfe Tone. (Also a lawyer, Tone later assisted the French in their invasion of Ireland in 1798. Condemned for treason, he cut his throat in prison.) On Tone's advice, Muir organised the FOTP into a dynamic force. Addressing meetings, he told his comrades 'we must act openly, actively and urgently!' and also urged:

ACT OPENLY, ACTIVELY AND URGENTLY... LIVE FREE OR DIE!

WAIT TILL THE SECRETARY OF STATE HEARS ABOUT THIS!

This was misinterpreted by government spies, and the authorities panicked, fearing armed insurrection. Arrested, Muir faced trial in Edinburgh in 1793 along with his accomplices **William Skirving** (a small landowner), the **Rev. Thomas Fyshe Palmer** (a Unitarian minister) and two activists from London, **Maurice Margarot** and **Joseph Gerrald**.

The trial was presided over by the notorious **Judge Braxfield**, a man noted for his ruthlessness and prejudice. He was known as the 'Judge Jeffreys of Scotland', a Scottish counterpart of England's notorious hanging judge, George Jeffreys (1648-1689), famed for his brutality and his immediate assumption of guilt of those he tried.

Braxfield's favourite phrase was 'Let them bring me prisoners and I'll find them law'. Ignoring 21 defence witnesses, he sentenced the prisoners to transportation: 14 years in the penal colony of New South Wales, Australia. In February 1794 the group was shipped off to Botany Bay, becoming known as the **'EDINBURGH MARTYRS'** (in Australia they are called the 'Scottish Martyrs'). Muir eventually escaped, however, with help from American and Spanish ships' captains, reaching revolutionary France, where he received a hero's welcome and was granted political asylum as an honorary citizen of the Republic.

Muir's transportation inspired **ROBERT BURNS** (1759-1796) to write the patriotic song 'Scots Wha Hae', commemorating Bannockburn. It was banned as seditious. His sympathy with the reform movement could have got him transported himself for treason and sedition, but he had useful contacts in court. Burns, Scotland's national poet, has been translated into many languages, but he wrote most of his most famous poems in Scots. Very much a 'man of the people' (he was himself a tenant farmer), his satire of hoity-toity members of the establishment and hypocritical members of the Kirk is sharp and witty. His sympathy lay always with the poor and oppressed and even extended to animals. He was a womanizer, but women loved him. Burns simply loved humanity.

While the Martyrs were being transported, the government suspended all laws against wrongful or unlawful imprisonment. This provoked further anger. A hidden armoury of pikes was discovered in Edinburgh in May 1794, belonging to revolutionaries hoping to distribute them in a bid to seize power. This was known as the **'PIKE PLOT'**. Two leaders, **David Downie** and **Robert Watt**, were arrested and tried for high treason. Downie was sentenced to transportation, Watt to be hanged and beheaded.

THE GOVERNMENT INTRODUCED THE MILITIA ACT (1797), CONSCRIPTING ALL MEN INTO PART-TIME MILITARY SERVICE TO CONTROL RIOTS. THOSE RICH ENOUGH, HOWEVER, COULD HIRE SUBSTITUTES TO TAKE THEIR PLACE.

THIS ONLY SPARKED OFF MORE RIOTING. AT TRANENT, NEAR PRESTONPANS, RIOTING MINERS (WHO REFUSED TO BE CALLED UP) AND THEIR FAMILIES WERE CRUSHED BY CHARGING CAVALRY WHO KILLED 12 PEOPLE INCLUDING A WOMAN AND A BOY OF 13.

Although the Friends of the People had stated in their declaration that they respected the law and the British constitution, the ruling class of the time had made it clear that they did not like the idea of representation of the people. The successor to the Friends of the People, therefore, had to organise in secret. This was the **UNITED SCOTSMEN** which campaigned for annual general elections as well as universal suffrage and Scottish home rule. Originally a reform group, it later became revolutionary. Indeed, there were three allied groups: the United Scotsmen, United Irishmen and United Englishmen, dedicated to establishing republics in Scotland, Ireland and England respectively.

GEORGE MEALMAKER, a radical handloom weaver from Dundee and leader of the United Scotsmen, had been active in the Friends of the People and had even written a manifesto for one of the transported Edinburgh martyrs, the minister Thomas Fyshe Palmer. Mealmaker had also been involved with a Dundee-based group called the Friends of Liberty from 1792 to 1793. The republican United Scotsmen had several branches spread throughout Fife and Angus, holding secret meetings in which delegates from each branch remained anonymous, known only by the names of their branches. Arrested for sedition himself in November 1797 for writing and publishing subversive pamphlets, Mealmaker went down for 14 years' transportation. His prosecutors gave reluctant compliments, amazed that a 'mere' weaver was capable of such intelligent literary talent.

In the early 19th century, following Britain's wars against revolutionary and Napoleonic France, civil unrest started up again, such as strikes and riots, as Scots faced unemployment, low wages and the lack of democratic representation. Change had to happen - it was in the air - and the upper classes were getting nervous. Things finally came to a head in 1820 with a workers' uprising in the Glasgow area and the west of Scotland: the 1820 **'RADICAL WAR'** - an insurrection in which workers organised themselves but which was brought down by undercover government infiltrators with instructions to find and remove the ringleaders.

Local leaders, actually encouraged by government spies, set up a 'Provisional Government', whose policies included separate parliaments for Scotland and England, universal adult suffrage and annual general elections. They published a poster, now believed to be the work of one of the government agents, posted on walls all over the west of Scotland. The poster, addressed 'To the inhabitants of Great Britain and Ireland', openly prompted armed revolution, the seizure of factories by workers, and mutiny in the army. It also informed people that the Provisional Government, which was now taking control, was planning a general strike and uprising, to commence on 1 April.

This had an immediate effect, with 60,000 people in Glasgow coming out on strike and troops lining the streets. What they did not realise was that secret arrests had been carried out, capturing 28 of the Provisional Government members (meetings had been infiltrated by government informants). A police report read that the arrested activists 'confessed their audacious plot to sever the Kingdom of Scotland from that of England and restore the ancient Scottish parliament'.

On the evening of 1 April, 300 radical followers clashed with cavalry, but there were no casualties. Radical organisation continued, however, with local units gathering in different parts of the city, collecting weapons and ammunition, and Glasgow Green was used as a training ground for the revolutionary army. Across Lanarkshire, local contingents collected arms and recruited new members.

In Strathaven, Lanarkshire, 60-year-old **JAMES WILSON** (1760-1820), a radical weaver and veteran of the Friends of the People (possibly the United Scotsmen as well) held a meeting of local militants in his house. The next day, Monday 2 April, the Strathaven militants prepared guns, ammunition and pikes, getting ready to join the revolt. A messenger arrived from Glasgow on 5 April with the news that all Lanarkshire radicals were planning to meet up the next day on the Cathkin Braes (just outside Glasgow). They were then to march on Glasgow and join up with radicals in the city for a full-scale attack on the British army. That evening, the Strathaven insurgents went round the town looking for more recruits and weapons.

Next morning, under a large red banner with the words SCOTLAND FREE OR A DESERT emblazoned upon it, 50 armed men left the town. The Strathaven contingent reached the Cathkin Braes, only to find themselves alone. No other units had arrived. They sent a messenger to Glasgow to find out whether there had been a change of plan and in the meantime raised their red flag on the Braes, overlooking the Clyde Valley with the city of Glasgow below. The messenger returned with the warning that troops and police had been alerted and were rounding up radicals, so they left as quickly as possible and dispersed in small groups. Wilson, however, was eventually captured.

Meanwhile, just outside Falkirk lay the Carron Iron Works, where government artillery and munitions were manufactured. Government agents instructed some Glasgow radicals to advance to Falkirk, where they would supposedly be joined by reinforcements, and to seize the Carron Iron Works. On arriving there on 5 April the radicals found that no other contingent had turned up. They then dispersed, 30 of them stopping to rest at Bonnymuir, where they were attacked by waiting units of hussars and yeomanry in the shoot-out now known as the **Battle of Bonnymuir**, Four radicals were wounded, 19 taken prisoner.

A few days later, on Saturday 8 April, the citizens of Greenock gathered in protest as 5 radical prisoners from Paisley were escorted to Greenock Gaol under armed escort by the Port Glasgow Militia, who fired on the crowd indiscriminately, killing 8 people, including boys - one only 8 years old - and wounding another 10, including a 65-year-old woman and a number of boys. That night, the Greenock people returned, stormed the Gaol and freed the prisoners, of whom only one was recaptured.

At his trial, James Wilson made the speech:

'You may condemn me to immolation on the scaffold, but you cannot degrade me. If I have appeared as a pioneer in the van of freedom's battles, if I have attempted to free my country from political degradation, my conscience tells me that I have only done my duty.'

Hardie and Baird were sent to Stirling Castle to be hanged in public. A protesting crowd cried 'Murder!' as the victims' heads were afterwards chopped off.

Wilson was similarly hanged and beheaded on Glasgow Green on Wednesday 30 August in front of a crowd of 20,000 people. 'Did you ever see such a crowd, Thomas?' he asked the executioner just before his death. The crowd, shouting 'Shame!' and 'He dies for his country!' were angry, sympathetic and driven to tears. It was a very emotional scene in which some - soldiers included - fainted

Heavy industry continued to grow as Scotland became an industrial nation. Dredging and deepening of the Clyde allowed ocean-going shipping to dock at Glasgow, which was to become the 'Workshop of the British Empire', building ships, locomotives and heavy engineering plant and machinery for use throughout the colonies.

In the early 19th century, children worked in the mines and factories with their parents, who earned just enough to pay the rent for their slum dwellings and to buy just enough food to keep them alive.

In the meantime, federated trades unions replaced the craft combinations, helping to raise political awareness among the people, as did the **CHARTISTS**, a UK-wide organisation which aimed to pressurise the government into democratic reform, laid out in the 'People's Charter', drawn up in 1838, from which they took their name. In some ways the demands of the Charter were a compromise compared with those of the Friends of the People and the United Scotsmen. They included annual general elections but not home rule, and universal *male* suffrage, giving the working man the right to vote but not women of any class. But working women were supportive and active in the movement, seeing it as a step in the right direction.

Strikes and clashes with employers or police were common throughout the rest of the century, but a series of Reform Acts (1832-1884) passed by Whig, Tory and Liberal governments under pressure from working-class action gradually introduced universal male suffrage although in practice, before 1918, fewer men in Scotland than in England could vote, because of registration. Women remained excluded, denied the right to vote until after the First World War. The unions would struggle for justice for everyone, and men did increasingly express support for women's votes through unions, local government and churches but, more significantly, women organised themselves. Women's meetings and activities, culminating in support for the Suffragette movement of the early 20th century, were held all over Scotland.

In 1903, **Helen Crawford** (later a co-founder of the Communist Party of Great Britain) and **Janie Allan** organised the Glasgow branch of the Women's Social and Political Union while, in London, **Flora 'Bluebell' Drummond** organised mass processions. Between 1908-1913, Glasgow Art School became a centre of feminist activity, and actresses **Annie Fraser** and **Maggie Moffat** became the first Scots to be arrested for furthering the Suffragette cause. By 1913, faced with the government's stubborn refusal to introduce votes for women, the movement turned violent. In a campaign known as the Scottish Outrages, letter boxes in Glasgow were acid-bombed by **Jessie Stephen's** Domestic Workers' Union while Farrington Hall in Dundee, a marine laboratory in St Andrews, the railway station at Leuchars and other buildings were burned down in protest.

MARY PHILLIPS (SCOTTISH SUFFRAGETTE) AFTER RELEASE FROM HOLLOWAY PRISON, 1908.

But the overall movement for democracy in Scotland remained inseparable from home rule, and important labour leaders of the turn of the century (such as miners' leaders Robert Smillie and James Keir Hardie) who campaigned for parliamentary reform and for women's suffrage were also supporters of the Scottish Home Rule Association.

ROBERT SMILLIE

At the end of the 19th century, Queen Victoria was on the throne and the British Empire was at the peak of its influence. Many Scots became imperialists, setting off to colonise, administer or police the Empire in Africa or India, keeping native peoples under control while companies exploited the colonies' natural resources. It offered career opportunities, no doubt.

At home, however, opposition to imperialism from the labour, liberal, trades union and nationalist movements would grow. Scotland developed rapidly at this time. The cities of Glasgow, Edinburgh, Dundee and Aberdeen grew; there were railways and canals linking the coalfields and industrial towns. But despite this economic (if environmentally unhealthy) prosperity, social divisions between rich and poor were very wide, while the demand for home rule remained strong. In 1886, the **Scottish Home Rule Association** was formed, based on an Irish example. A Liberal MP, **R.B. Cunninghame-Grahame**, a London-born Scot, became its first President.

At this time, many people invested their hopes and votes in the **LIBERAL PARTY**, seen then as the party of reform, in opposition to the hard-line Tory or Conservative Party, which resisted change. The Liberal Party was also the party of home rule. Liberal Leader **William Ewart Gladstone** proposed devolved parliaments for Ireland and Scotland. But both the first and second Home Rule Bills were defeated in Parliament.

WILLIAM GLADST...

In the early years of the 20th century, Welsh Liberal MP **David Lloyd George** again took up the matter in the House of Commons. One of the founders of Cymru Fydd (Young Wales), Lloyd George demanded 'Home Rule all round'. When asked by an opponent 'How about Home Rule for Hell?' he replied 'Certainly! Let every man speak for his own country!'. But again proposals in Parliament were repeatedly dropped, and Lloyd George eventually lost interest in the matter, even after becoming Prime Minister in 1916. The cause of home rule would be taken up by another force...

DAVID LLOYD GEORGE

JAMES KEIR HARDIE (1856-1915), Ayrshire miners' leader, formed the Independent Labour Party (independent of the Liberals, that is), which eventually joined with other organisations to become the **LABOUR PARTY**. The idea was to establish a people's party which would be sponsored by the trades unions and would effectively represent them in Parliament.

On self-government, Keir Hardie wrote:

'I wonder why it is that some men oppose home rule for the land of their birth.'

And again:

'When the men elected to make laws are a small part of a foreign parliament, all national feeling dies...I have always been a strong supporter of self-government.'

Keir Hardie was a strong champion of home rule for Scotland and Wales, but he never lived to see a Labour government. He was, however, Britain's first Labour MP becoming MP for Merthyr Tydfil, Wales, in

Between the forming of the Scottish Home Rule Association in 1886 and the beginning of World War I in 1914, the matter of Scottish home rule was raised in Parliament on 13 occasions and rejected each time. Following the Irish Treaty of 1921, giving home rule to Ireland and to Northern Ireland, Socialist MP for Glasgow Gorbals, **George Buchanan**, introduced the Federal Home Rule Bill.

Up to the 1923 general election, the Labour Party actively and strongly supported home rule as an official policy and a democratic

necessity. Scottish votes helped bring Labour to power in 1923, but Labour's first Prime Minister, Scotsman **Ramsay MacDonald** (1866-1937), faced with economic crisis, was forced to compromise his policies, forming a coalition with the Conservatives and Liberals. Once again, the issue of Scottish self-government was dropped in Parliament, this time for nearly half a century.

When the home rule issue was dropped in Parliament in 1923, others felt provoked into taking the matter a stage further, campaigning not merely for autonomy but for full independence.

This gave rise to the independence or 'Nationalist' movement, as it is commonly known. But the word 'nationalism' can be a bit misleading as it might imply building barriers between people, as opposed to internationalism. Yet one of the first people in the 20th century to campaign for Scottish independence was a staunch internationalist.

JOHN MACLEAN (1879-1923), Clydeside socialist, equated international workers' power with the need to bring down imperialism, particularly the British Empire which was then the leading world power.

Evicted crofters cleared from their Highland home, MacLean's parents settled in the south side of Glasgow. His father worked in a pottery, dying of illness contracted through the dusty working conditions.

JOHN MACLEAN

Graduating from Glasgow University, MacLean became a schoolteacher but resolved to use his education to change the fortunes of the working class. Teaching schoolchildren by day, he also ran a weekly adult night school. The lessons, however, were not in orthodox academic subjects but in working-class history, Marxist economics and revolutionary socialism.

Many important trades union leaders and 'Red Clydeside' Labour and Communist MPs in the inter-war years had been students at MacLean's evening class, such as the fiery left-wing Independent Labour MP James Maxton.

John MacLean remains to this day a Glasgow folk hero and an icon of the Scottish (indeed, British) trades union movement.

A Marxist revolutionary, he organised the Upper Clyde shipyard workers and trades union on Clydeside into a dynamic force. He was founder of the Scottish Labour College. He formed the Clyde Workers' Committee, organised strikes and workers' organisations and institutions, attempting to encourage non-violent revolution. He campaigned for price reductions, a minimum wage, a 6-hour day, rationing of work and payment of full wages to the unemployed.

When the Russian Bolshevik government offered to make him Soviet consul in Glasgow, he was seen as a threat to British national security and was imprisoned 5 times during and after the First World War, a war which he and his fellow Red Clydesiders opposed and in which 147,609 Scots died - a fifth of Britain's dead! Yet he refused to join the Communist Party of Great Britain, rejecting its centralism and party authority.

World War I (1914-1918) was a tragic waste of human life as thousands of Scots died in the trenches of the 'Western Front', on the borders of France, Belgium and Germany.

> How did the war start?
> (Briefly, please).

> The crown Prince of Austria was assassinated by Serbian nationalists. Austria declared war on Serbia. Russia and France allied with Serbia. Germany, Austria's ally, invaded Belgium. Britain and her Empire declared war on Germany.

At first there were plenty of volunteers, until news of the thousands of deaths came home, so conscription was introduced. British commanders kept trying to launch large-scale 'surprise attacks' on the Germans, who easily mowed down their enemy attackers with machine guns.

At home, many socialist trades unionists saw the war as merely a fight for control by Europe's ruling classes. Visiting Glasgow in 1915 and 1916, Prime Minister David Lloyd George met angry protest from some groups. In 1917 the **Scottish Trades Union Congress** (STUC) carried a unanimous resolution to call for peace negotiations. A Convention of Workers' and Soldiers' Councils was held in Glasgow on 11 August.

In March 1918, the STUC demanded a 40-hour week (without a cut in pay) to prevent high unemployment when the war ended.

After the war, the demand continued and, in January 1919, 40,000 workers went on strike in Glasgow. 6 tanks, 100 army lorries and 12,000 troops were sent to the city and stationed, in case of outbreak of red revolution.

On 31 January, a huge crowd mobbed George Square outside the City Chambers, where strike leaders **David Kirkwood** and **Emmanuel Shinwell** were trying to negotiate with the Lord Provost. A red flag was raised and a police-manned tram overturned. The police returned with mounted reinforcements wielding batons, 'clearing' the demonstration.

The Labour movement in Scotland up to 1923 demanded a Scottish parliament with economic ownership and control (not merely 'tax-varying powers' like today's Scottish Parliament). But John MacLean became disillusioned with the British labour movement, believing that socialism was more likely in an independent Scotland than in a united Britain.

'The social revolution is possible sooner in Scotland rather than in England... Scottish separation is part of the process of England's imperial disintegration and is a help towards the ultimate triumph of the workers of the world.'

Separate (but closely allied) Scottish and English republics would eventually be established, he hoped, and the workers of both countries would share the same trades union movement.

He formed the Scottish Workers Republican Party on his release from prison at the end of the First World War, with the aim of establishing a 'Socialist Republic of Scotland', with Glasgow as the capital.

John MacLean died of pneumonia (probably contracted while in prison) in 1923. He had spent four of the last eight years of his life in jail. 5000 people attended his funeral. To the end, his support for Scottish independence remained consistent with his internationalism. After all, why shouldn't it?

Another Marxist, but outside the mainstream movement because of his sentimental patriotism, was the poet **Hugh Macdiarmid** (1892-1978), who tried to start a revival of literature in the Scots tongue. He succeeded, but the Scots he used in his own poetry was actually a mixture of different dialects from various parts of Scotland.

HUGH MACDIARMID

MacDiarmid held that culture was essential to a small nation's identity. Without identity, a people cease to be a 'nation' and become absorbed into a larger culture, ultimately losing its political autonomy. In this way, he felt, Scottish culture was being eroded by English culture and this helped sustain England's hegemony over Scotland.

MacDiarmid joined the National Party of Scotland as one of its founder members, but was expelled because of his communist views. He then joined the Communist Party of Great Britain, but they expelled him for his Scottish nationalist views!

The National Party, formed in 1928 by Rhuiraidh Erskine of Marr out of a fusion of nationalist groups, came about partly in response to the apparent abandonment at that time by the labour, liberal and socialist movements of home rule, and partly out of sympathy with the Irish republicans, who had at least obtained independence for all but six northern counties of Ireland. Indeed, one of the leaders of the Easter Rising in Ireland in 1916, **James Connolly** (1868-1916), was a Scotsman from Edinburgh. A socialist with views similar to John MacLean, he was executed by firing squad for his part in the uprising. Unable to stand because of a leg injury, he was shot tied to a chair.

In its early days, the National Party emphasised ethnic Celtic awareness with an anti-English resentment, giving themselves a regrettable anglophobic reputation which cost them popular support. Later, as the **SCOTTISH NATIONAL PARTY** (SNP), a more international outlook and a policy of multicultural, non-racial, civic nationalism would be adopted, along with an 'open border' policy (i.e. no passport or immigration controls with England after independence).

The years between the wars are well-associated with economic hardship. Britain's 10-day General Strike (1926) in support of miners, who were having to work longer hours for less pay, was beaten. The Great Depression of the 1930s brought anti-unemployment and hunger marches and the emigration of 400,000 Scots.

In 1939, when Hitler invaded Poland, Britain declared war on Germany. Thus the Second World War (1939-1945) began with Britain, USA, France and the USSR against Germany, Italy and Japan. During the War, Nazi propagandists sent radio messages to Scotland, trying to appeal to Scottish national awareness to turn against the British government. Not a chance!

The Luftwaffe meanwhile bombed towns and city areas throughout Scotland, particularly Clydebank where, during the blackout, they missed their intended target, the shipyards, hitting the housing area.

The Highlands and Islands were used by the British government to test experimental weapons, including bacteriological warfare, leaving certain places uninhabitable.

The war ended in August 1945. 57,720 Scots had been killed.

After the war, Britain's economic boom meant that British industry was making money and Scotland's trades unions (which had by now become branches of British trades unions with headquarters in London) could demand their share. Some in the Scottish labour movement lost enthusiasm for home rule, seeing it as potentially dividing the strength of the British labour movement. Others, however, would eventually persuade the STUC to campaign for a Scottish parliament.

Despite faith in **Clement Atlee's** government, Scottish national awareness was to revive. On Christmas Day 1950, the Stone of Destiny was seized from Westminster Abbey by a group of Scottish students led by Ian Hamilton (who later became a QC), causing outrage in the English Press, who described the act as 'theft'.

WE WERE ONLY TAKING BACK WHAT WAS STOLEN FROM US.

The Stone was returned to Westminster after negotiation.

In 1952, pillar boxes in Scotland bearing the new Queen's initials (EIIR) were blasted with gelignite or otherwise destroyed as one of several small acts of protest by the Scottish Patriots, led by **Wendy Wood**. (The Queen was Elizabeth II of England, not of Scotland where, strictly speaking, she was Elizabeth I.)

But such stunts were only expressions of 'petty' nationalism with emotional rather than political aims, meant to ensure the survival of national identity, and were not directly concerned with the issue of home rule.

More to the point was the **SCOTTISH COVENANT**, organised by a Glasgow lawyer, **John MacCormick**, in 1949. This was a petition to the British government, signed by over 2 million people (two-thirds of the Scottish electorate), demanding home rule. But Parliament ruled that such a constitutional change could not be brought about by a petition, and rejected the matter.

SCOTTISH COVENANT
SIGN HERE IF YOU WANT TO SEE A SCOTTISH PARLIAMENT

Successive British governments under Atlee and Macmillan were opposed to any form of devolution or home rule, deeming it unnecessary in a booming postwar Britain. For a time, everyone enjoyed the benefits of free healthcare, student grants, the welfare state and public funding for schools and council housing. But Scotland's traditional industries were becoming outdated and its economy was controlled by financiers who developed English industries but thought it needless to modernise old industries in Scotland which still made a profit in the short term. Scots voted against **Harold Macmillan's** government in the general election of 1959 but English votes put the Conservatives back in power, as they would in 1970 with Edward Heath, throughout the 1980s with Margaret Thatcher, and in the 1990s with John Major. This lack of democratic control over Scotland's own affairs heralded a rising tide of nationalism, fuelled also by dissatisfaction over worsening economic conditions. The SNP began to make gains, sending MPs to Parliament (the SNP's first MP, **Winnie Ewing**, was elected in Hamilton in 1967). It was clearly more than a 'protest vote' as people could have voted for opposition parties other than the SNP.

I'LL GIVE INDIA HOME RULE BUT NOT SCOTLAND.

CLEMENT ATTLEE

As British imperialism declined and foreign competition rose, overseas markets were lost and Britain sank into recession in the 1970s. When the Upper Clyde Shipbuilders yards were threatened with closure in 1971, 80,000 people marched in protest in Glasgow and 200,000 Scots stopped work in sympathy. Led by shop stewards **Jimmy Reid** and **Jimmy Airlie**, the yard workers locked themselves in and carried on working. The 'work-in' lasted 16 months until Edward Heath's Tory government backed down. (Jimmy Reid would tell *The Herald* newspaper years later: 'All my life I have dreamed of the day when Scotland would have its own parliament'.)

New hope arrived for Scotland with the discovery of oil under Scottish waters of the North Sea. Scotland was now an oil-producing country but, unlike other oil-producing countries, one which got poorer. The massive revenues from the oil wealth flowed southwards, making little difference to Scotland's surging unemployment or economic problems. The consequent rise of nationalist support brought the SNP to the position of Scotland's second main political party, at least in terms of votes cast (second, that is, to Labour).

Faced with nationalist rivalry, Scottish Labour MPs pressed their party into a momentous decision: a revived commitment to home rule for Scotland.

chapter 6
devolution delayed

In 1974, **Harold Wilson's** Labour government pledged 'devolution' of power from London, with a Scottish mini-parliament or 'assembly' in Edinburgh, firmly within the UK but with delegated responsibilities. This won Labour the October general election of that year and another term in office (though the SNP made startling gains, returning 11 MPs - the most they would ever send to the UK Parliament), but it was soon revealed that the assembly's powers would be limited to those already exercised by local authorities (e.g. school education, water, gas, housing, etc.).

LET'S MAKE SURE THEY DON'T HAVE ANY MORE CONTROL THAN THEY ALREADY HAVE.

A GLORIFIED LOCAL COUNCIL!

The state, meanwhile, fearing seizure of oil platforms by Scottish terrorists, had special troops trained in anti-guerrilla action. There were a few incidents, unsupported by the public, such as bomb attacks in 1975 by the so-called **Army of the Provisional Government** ('Tartan Army') on oil pipelines, but fortunately no harm to human life.

The Scots were to decide on whether or not they wanted an assembly by voting in a referendum, delayed until 1979, just before the next general election. The government meanwhile did not strongly press for or encourage a favourable vote, and the SNP's support was cautious.

By the time the referendum came around the Scottish voters were rather lost. Disillusioned by further economic stagnation, lacking a united, organised leadership, they became increasingly sceptical of the whole devolution affair. The government demanded a minimum level of 40% of the electorate to vote in favour before an assembly would be granted. But turnout on polling day was poor. Of those who did vote, a majority voted in favour, but it wasn't enough to pass the required limit.

Afterwards the Tories (opposed to home rule) declared a Vote of No Confidence in the government. The SNP - much to the cost of their own public support and credibility at the time - unwisely voted with them, bringing down the Labour government. A general election ensued, the result of which, against the stated wishes of the majority of the people of Scotland, was that **Margaret Thatcher** was brought to power in 1979, largely by votes in the English South East and Midlands.

Once in office, Thatcher was seen as a new 'Hammer of the Scots', as the policies she carried out proved unwelcome there.

The Conservative government's agenda included tax cuts, limits on trades union powers and privatisation of industry, but these policies were viewed by most Scots as alien. For example, government policy was to stop handing out funds to ailing or uncompetitive industries and businesses. To the Scots, who were often dependent on government subsidy to keep factories working, this meant the closure of many workplaces.

Meanwhile, Scotland's crime rate (particularly drug-related crime) increased throughout the 1980s and 1990s, as did health problems, with Scotland reaching the highest rates in Britain for lung cancer, heart disease and tooth decay.

Political opponents and moderates in Mrs Thatcher's own party protested at the toughness of her policies, warning of the social consequences, but the Prime Minister remained unmoved. Her popularity in Scotland, already low, dropped even further in the face of a rising demand for home rule.

Home rule, however, was out of the question for the time being. Thatcher had declared early on that there would be no Scottish Assembly as long as she was Prime Minister and, following the referendum, the 1978 Scotland Act was repealed.

When cheaper (but more environmentally harmful) coal began to be imported from Colombia and South Africa, Scottish miners joined the National Miners' Strike (February 1984-March 1985) against pit closures. After a long and bitter struggle, the miners were defeated and all but one of Scotland's coal mines closed. The one remaining open was kept only to supply Longannet power station, near Kincardine. Another pit, Monktonhall Colliery in Lothian, was bought by the miners themselves, who tried to run it as a private mine, but the business eventually failed, unable to compete in the international market.

COAL NOT DOLE
SAVE SCOTTISH PITS

Through government policy, either by direct closure or lack of subsidy or assistance, many major factories closed, as well as mines and shipyards. Scotland quickly became de-industrialised.

LET'S TRY IT OUT ON THE SCOTS FIRST.

What was widely seen in Scotland as a final insult was the Poll Tax (or Community Charge, as it was officially called). A system of local taxation whereby everyone, rich or poor, had to pay the same rates, it was hated and condemned by many as unfair to people on lower incomes. In Glasgow, a protest march of 40,000 people was held. A million Scots refused to pay up, even though their belongings could be seized and sold in warrant sales.

But perhaps what most angered people was the way the government used Scotland as a testing ground, trying out the system on the Scots for a year before inflicting it on the rest of the UK. (Scottish Conservatives had in fact begged Thatcher to do so, though it was to prove the biggest blow to their own party in Scotland.)

The Poll Tax was continued, like all of Thatcher's other hard-line policies, by **John Major**, who succeeded her as Conservative Prime Minister in 1990. By the end of the following year, around 240,000 houses were spoiled with damp while council house building had virtually stopped and homelessness had almost doubled in over 4 years.

JOHN MAJOR

ANNABEL GOLDIE
(A LEADING SCOTS TORY)

THE CONSERVATIVES ARE THE GOVERNMENT OF SCOTLAND.

AYE. UNELECTED GOVERNMENT.

Local councils were forced to carry out the Poll Tax, but Glasgow councillor **Tommy Sheridan** of Scottish Militant Labour encouraged his constituents to refuse to pay. He brought about the cancellation of a warrant sale, breaching a court order and was imprisoned for 5 months in 1992, during which time he conducted election campaigns from his cell in Saughton prison, Edinburgh (this was subsequently made illegal) and gave media interviews. After his sentence, he returned to Glasgow to a tumultuous welcome, and was carried shoulder high from Queen Street Station to the City Chambers. However, the Council was determined to act within the law, and Sheridan's campaign was depriving it of funds. Poll Tax implementation and warrant sales continued. Sheridan later formed the left wing, pro-independence Scottish Socialist Party (1998), campaigning in the 1999 Scottish Parliament election.

I AM NOT A NUMBER, I AM A FREE MAN!

PRESS

TOMMY SHERIDAN

No-loans

NO POLL TAX

THE LAW WILL SOON PUT A STOP TO THIS!

When the Conservatives won the general election again in 1992 the Scots, sickened by 13 years of unwanted rule imposed on them by a government they had voted against, knew it would mean another 5 years of hardship. This was a turning point. Opposition parties in Scotland united as never before, the Scottish Trades Union Congress and the Labour, SNP and Liberal Democrat parties jointly formed the **SCOTLAND UNITED** campaign, whose aim was to press the government to hold a referendum in Scotland on its constitutional future, demanding that the Scots be given the choice of devolution, independence or the status quo. John Major refused to give the matter any consideration, perhaps knowing and fearing the outcome.

On 12 December 1992, Major was in Edinburgh at a European summit meeting in Holyrood Palace, (at which Scotland had no independent representation), when a protest march of 25,000 people, organised jointly by the STUC and Scotland United, marched past on Calton Hill. He arrogantly disregarded it as 'an irrelevance'.

The march started from outside the old Royal High School on Calton Hill, the original location for the proposed assembly. It continued through the city centre, ending up at at The Meadows, where an agreement was signed between Labour, the SNP and Liberal Democrats, pledging that their Scottish MPs would recall and set up a Scottish parliament if the government refused to give way.

But Scottish Labour MP **Henry McLeish**, who had signed the pact, was ordered by party headquarters in London to withdraw as the action might jeopardize their chances of winning the next general election. McLeish's co-signatory, SNP leader **Alex Salmond**, accused him of reneging, but Labour had plans to hold a referendum in Scotland within a year of office (once elected) on the matter of a Scottish parliament, which they themselves would encourage. The parliament would have stronger powers than the 'assembly' proposed back in the 1970s, including a limited amount of tax-raising power, at least on incomes if not on industries.

Labour leader **John Smith** died suddenly in 1994, to be replaced by **Tony Blair**, who immediately reformed the party into 'New Labour'. Hoping to gain crucial votes, he 'modernised' his party's policies, adopting a less socialist stance than 'Old' Labour had pursued.

Meanwhile, Scottish Labour and Scottish Liberal Democrats forged another joint campaign: **SCOTLAND FORWARD.**

The aim of this would be to encourage Scottish voters to support a devolved Scottish parliament, within the UK, in the promised referendum. When it was declared that the option of independence would not be included, the SNP witheld support for the time being.

But mainstream Scottish opinion supported devolution, including many people who sought independence, as they saw devolution as a realistic first step in an ongoing process of self-government.

JIM SILLARS, DEPUTY SNP LEADER TOOK 'INDEPENDENCE-OR-NOTHING' STANCE, URGING NON-COOPERATION WITH SCOTLAND FORWARD

Labour's Shadow Secretary of State for Scotland, **George Robertson**, denounced the SNP as 'separatists' and 'anti-English'. Alex Salmond, whose party in fact included English members and activists, doubted Labour's sincerity and commitment towards home rule. While Labour had taken a rightward turn from their traditional line of policies, the SNP had adopted a left-of-centre stance, and the party purged itself of any anti-English groups or elements.

> A STRONG SCOTTISH PARLIAMENT, FIRMLY WITHIN AND STRENGTHENING THE UK, WILL KILL SEPARATISM STONE DEAD.

GORGE BERTSON

ALEX SALMOND

> WE WANT THE SCOTTISH PARLIAMENT TO WORK. WE HOPE IT WILL GIVE THE SCOTTISH PEOPLE SELF-CONFIDENCE.

On St Andrew's Day (30 November) 1996, John Major returned the Stone of Destiny to Scotland (today it rests in Edinburgh Castle as a public exhibit), hoping to win support in Scotland in the coming general election.

IF I GIVE THEM THEIR STONE BACK, MAYBE THEY'LL REMEMBER WHAT A NICE BLOKE I AM WHEN THEY GO TO VOTE.

THE SCOTS WOULD PROBABLY HAVE EVENTUALLY DEMANDED ITS RETURN TO SCOTLAND ANYWAY!

But most Scots, nationalists included, were unimpressed by the token gesture.

WE NEED LESS OF THE SYMBOL AND MORE OF THE SUBSTANCE.

When the 1997 general election arrived, Labour at last swept to victory, winning by a landslide. In Scotland, the few Conservative seats were all lost to parties supporting home rule.

On becoming Prime Minister, Tony Blair carried on many policies introduced by the Conservatives. However, he did not go back on his pledge to hold a referendum in Scotland on the home rule issue. **Donald Dewar** was appointed as Scottish Secretary of State, whose duties would include setting up the parliament should the results of the referendum prove favourable. But the management of the referendum itself was delegated to Henry McLeish, who was now Scottish Home Affairs Minister.

DONALD DEWAR

Everything was now set for the historic referendum.

The SNP finally joined the Scotland Forward campaign in time for the referendum, forming a much-needed unity between Scotland's three main political parties. The referendum was put to the people of Scotland on 11 September 1997. As the results poured in, it was clear - verifying predictions based on opinion polls - that the Scots wanted a Scottish parliament with tax-raising powers. A triumphant mood swept across Scotland that night. After nearly three centuries, a Scottish parliament was to be restored, forming the biggest constitutional change in Scottish history since the Act of Union.

A cross-party vigil, manned for 24 hours a day for five years at Calton Hill, Edinburgh, outside the proposed assembly building was particularly jubilant. But Donald Dewar decided on a new site, near Holyrood Palace. On 19 November 1998, the Scotland Act was passed by the UK Parliament. Devolution became law.

The new Parliament building, resembling upturned boats and designed by the Spanish architect Enrico Miralles, would not be ready until 2001, but the Parliament had to be in operation by 1999, with elections held in May. Temporary accommodation therefore had to be found, so the Church of Scotland offered use of its Assembly Halls on The Mound, in the centre of the capital.

The location of the new building having been chosen, plans for how the new Parliament would work were thought out.

SCOTTISH PARLIAMENT BUILDING, HOLYROOD, EDINBURGH

In Scotland, the population is 52% female yet, in the UK Parliament of 650 (of which 72 MPs represent Scotland), only 12 Scottish MPs were female at the time of the legislation of the new Scottish Parliament (1998). Therefore, women constituted 16% of Scotland's MPs.

It was hoped that the Scottish parliament would ultimately have equal representation for both sexes, and the Scottish Labour Party resolved to submit equal numbers of male and female candidates in the 1999 election for the Scottish Parliament, as a move towards this aim.

It was further hoped that ethnic minorities would also be represented, and the main parties planned to put up more candidates from ethnic minority groups, because the national issue is a civic, not a racial or ethnic, issue. Anyone living permanently in Scotland, regardless of their birthplace, ancestry or national/ethnic origin, is a Scot.

It was hoped that the new Scottish Parliament would be fairer and more democratic than the Westminster Parliament had been. It was decided that the Scottish Parliament would operate partly on a traditional 'first-past-the-post' system (like the UK Parliament), and partly on proportional representation (PR) whereby each party's number of MSPs would correspond to the number of votes cast.

I DON'T FOLLOW.

Under 'first-past-the-post', the party with the biggest number of votes forms the government. Under proportional representation, each party's percentage of the total number of MSPs corresponds to the percentage of total votes they get. Okay?

THINK SO.

OTHER

LIBERAL DEM

CONSERVATIVE

SNP

LABOUR

SCOTTISH VOTERS

WE'LL DECIDE HOW THE CAKE IS DIVIDED.

However, challenges remain: unemployment, homelessness, poverty, etc.

The Scottish Parliament does not have the power to make any laws or constitutional changes regarding its own people without the consent or approval of the government in London. It does not have an independent voice in the European Council of Ministers, or a delegate to the Commonwealth Heads of Government meeting (even if the meeting is held in Scotland), or a seat in the United Nations.

Scotland's economy is controlled from outside, with many of its largest companies based in London or elsewhere outside Scotland.

The Parliament does not have full economic control. It may raise tax from people's incomes but not from industry, and especially not the all-important oil industry. It cannot make constitutional changes such as the abolition of the monarchy in Scotland (should the Scots so choose) or aristocratic titles. It cannot make decisions regarding defence, such as nuclear disarmament or neutrality during war.

But all these important Scottish issues can now be debated on Scottish soil. Future developments such as further oil prospecting, incentives for industrial and agricultural development, tax incentives for writers and artists, etc. are some of the issues addressed by Scotland's political parties.

159

Now that the people of Scotland have their own Parliament, they are able to choose their own destiny, whether autonomy within a more united federal Britain or independence in Europe on an equal partnership basis with other European nations. If Europe were to move towards becoming itself a federation, Scotland would have to decide between direct self-government in Europe or indirect self-government in Britain in Europe; an equal partner like France or Germany or a region like Bavaria or Catalonia.

Scotland must now look ahead towards economic and industrial development, such as the continuing search for new oilfields, support for Scotland's farmers and fishermen, and the expansion of Scotland's thriving financial services and high-technology industries; Scotland already produces nearly 40% of Europe's brand-name PCs and is home to five of the world's top eight computer manufacturers. With government incentives and a degree of economic planning, innovative new industries can also be established.

With Scotland's rich heritage, it is hoped that the arrival of the Scottish Parliament will reinforce the country's self-confidence and further develop its undoubted potential.

chronology

84	Battle of Mons Graupius. Romans defeat Picts, then withdraw southward.
503	Scots arrive (from Ireland) in Dalriada.
563	St Columba arrives in Iona.
843	Kenneth MacAlpin becomes King of Picts and Scots.
1292	Edward I of England conquers Scotland.
1297	Battle of Stirling Bridge.
1305	Execution of William Wallace.
1306	Robert the Bruce crowned King of Scotland.
1314	Battle of Bannockburn.
1320	Declaration of Arbroath.
1411	Founding of St Andrews University.
1472	Orkney and Shetland annexed.
1507	Printing press introduced into Scotland
1513	Battle of Flodden.
1587	Mary Queen of Scots executed.
1603	Union of Crowns.
1638	Signing of the National Covenant.
1643	Signing of the Solemn League and Covenant.
1653	Oliver Cromwell forces a union of Scotland and England.
1660	Restoration of Monarchy (and Scottish independence).
1688	Stuart monarchy deposed.
1689	Battle of Killiecrankie.
1692	Glencoe massacre.
1695	Bank of Scotland founded.
1698	Darien expedition.
1707	Union of Parliaments.
1715	Jacobite uprising led by Earl of Mar.
1724	General Wade appointed Commander-in-Chief of armed forces in 'North Britain'.
1745	Charles Edward Stuart leads last Jacobite uprising.
1746	Battle of Culloden.

1769	James Watt patents improved steam engine.
1770	River Clyde deepened to accommodate shipping: Glasgow becomes major port and industrial/commercial city.
1771	Encyclopaedia Britannica first issued, Edinburgh.
1776	Adam Smith's 'Wealth of Nations' published.
1790	Forth and Clyde Canal opened, linking Glasgow and Grangemouth (near Edinburgh).
1793	Trial of Thomas Muir.
1820	'Radical War'.
1885	Office of Secretary for Scotland created (elevated to that of Secretary of State for Scotland, 1926).
1890	Forth Rail Bridge built.
1897	Scottish Trades Union Congress formed.
1900	Labour Party formed. James Keir Hardie becomes first Labour MP.
1914-1918	World War I.
1919	'Forty Hours' strike and George Square demonstration, Glasgow.
1923	Ramsay MacDonald elected Prime Minister.
1928	Scottish National Party formed. Penicillin discovered.
1939-1945	World War II.
1949	Signing of the Scottish Covenant.
1967	Winifred Ewing becomes first Nationalist MP.
1971	'Work-in' at Upper Clyde Shipyards.
1975	Oil from the North Sea first piped ashore.
1979	Referendum on devolution (Scotland and Wales Act).
1985	Scottish coal industry closed.
1992	'Scotland United' formed. Home rule march and demonstration in Edinburgh.
1996	Stone of Destiny returned to Scotland.
1997	Referendum on Scottish Parliament. Majority of voters strongly in favour of home rule.
1998	Scotland Act passed by UK Parliament.
1999	Opening of Scottish Parliament.

genealogy

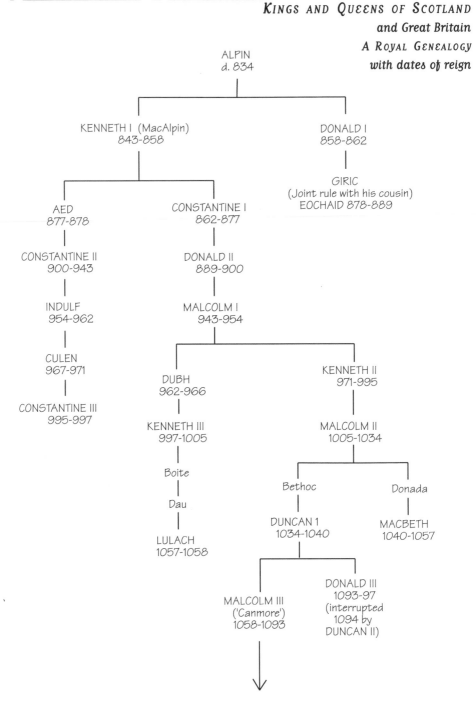

ALPIN
d. 834

KENNETH I (MacAlpin)
843-858

DONALD I
858-862

GIRIC
(Joint rule with his cousin)
EOCHAID 878-889

AED
877-878

CONSTANTINE I
862-877

CONSTANTINE II
900-943

DONALD II
889-900

INDULF
954-962

MALCOLM I
943-954

CULEN
967-971

DUBH
962-966

KENNETH II
971-995

CONSTANTINE III
995-997

KENNETH III
997-1005

MALCOLM II
1005-1034

Boite

Bethoc

Donada

Dau

DUNCAN 1
1034-1040

MACBETH
1040-1057

LULACH
1057-1058

MALCOLM III
('Canmore')
1058-1093

DONALD III
1093-97
(interrupted
1094 by
DUNCAN II)

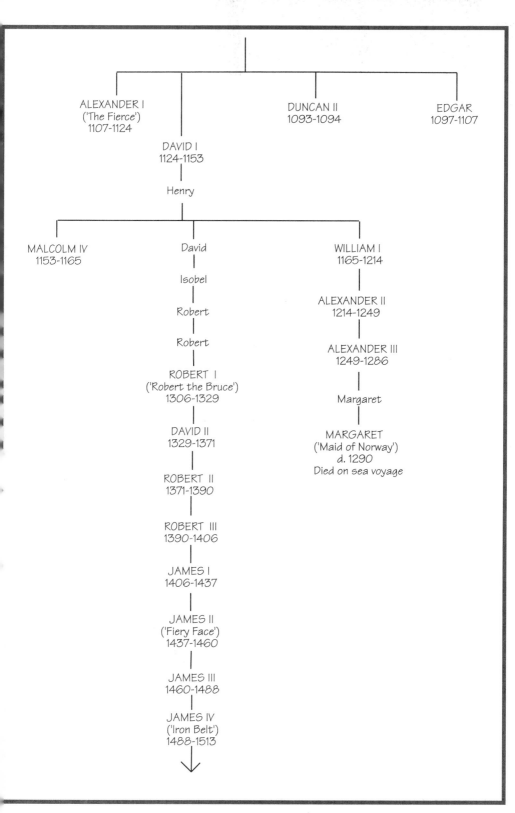

ALEXANDER I
('The Fierce')
1107-1124

DUNCAN II
1093-1094

EDGAR
1097-1107

DAVID I
1124-1153

Henry

MALCOLM IV
1153-1165

David

WILLIAM I
1165-1214

Isobel

ALEXANDER II
1214-1249

Robert

ALEXANDER III
1249-1286

Robert

ROBERT I
('Robert the Bruce')
1306-1329

Margaret

DAVID II
1329-1371

MARGARET
('Maid of Norway')
d. 1290
Died on sea voyage

ROBERT II
1371-1390

ROBERT III
1390-1406

JAMES I
1406-1437

JAMES II
('Fiery Face')
1437-1460

JAMES III
1460-1488

JAMES IV
('Iron Belt')
1488-1513

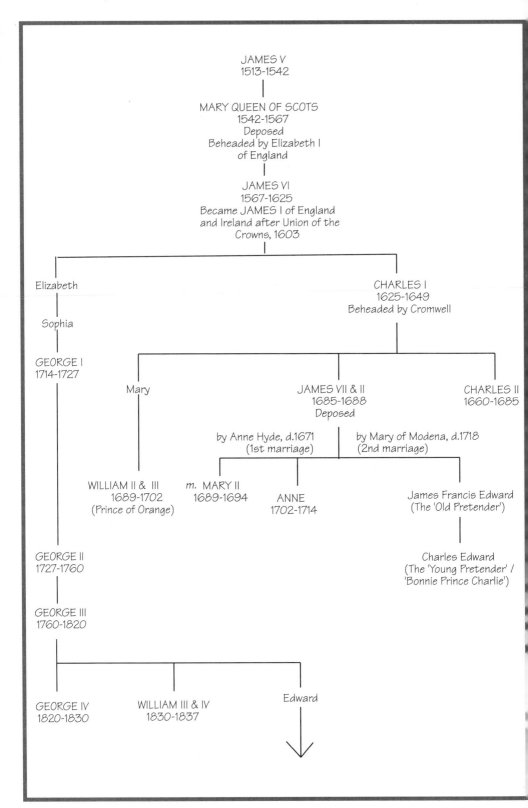

JAMES V
1513-1542

MARY QUEEN OF SCOTS
1542-1567
Deposed
Beheaded by Elizabeth I
of England

JAMES VI
1567-1625
Became JAMES I of England
and Ireland after Union of the
Crowns, 1603

Elizabeth

Sophia

GEORGE I
1714-1727

CHARLES I
1625-1649
Beheaded by Cromwell

Mary

JAMES VII & II
1685-1688
Deposed

CHARLES II
1660-1685

by Anne Hyde, d.1671
(1st marriage)

by Mary of Modena, d.1718
(2nd marriage)

WILLIAM II & III
1689-1702
(Prince of Orange)

m. MARY II
1689-1694

ANNE
1702-1714

James Francis Edward
(The 'Old Pretender')

GEORGE II
1727-1760

Charles Edward
(The 'Young Pretender' /
'Bonnie Prince Charlie')

GEORGE III
1760-1820

GEORGE IV
1820-1830

WILLIAM III & IV
1830-1837

Edward

166

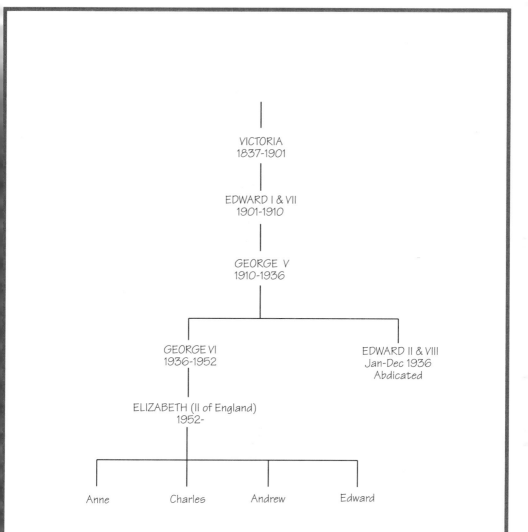

VICTORIA
1837-1901

EDWARD I & VII
1901-1910

GEORGE V
1910-1936

GEORGE VI
1936-1952

EDWARD II & VIII
Jan-Dec 1936
Abdicated

ELIZABETH (II of England)
1952-

Anne   Charles   Andrew   Edward

famous scots

INVENTION, INNOVATION & DISCOVERY

ANTISEPTIC Joseph Lister
CHLOROFORM ANAESTHESIS Sir James Young Simpson
IMPROVED STEAM ENGINE James Watt
MATHEMATICAL LOGARITHMS John Napier
PEDAL BICYCLE Kirkpatrick MacMillan
PENICILLIN Sir Alexander Fleming
PNEUMATIC TYRES Robert William Thomson, developed by John Boyd Dunlop
RADAR Sir Robert Alexander Watson-Watt
REAPING MACHINE Rev. Patrick Bell
REFLECTING TELESCOPE James Gregory
TARMAC John Loudon MacAdam
TELEVISION John Logie Baird
TELEPHONE Alexander Graham Bell
THRESHING MACHINE Andrew Meikle
VACUUM CLEANER Hubert Cecil Booth
VACUUM FLASK Sir James Dewar

EXPLORATION

AFRICA (the Niger) Mungo Park
AFRICA (the Blue Nile) James Bruce
AFRICA (the Zambezi/Lake Victoria) David Livingstone
ANTARTICA William Spiers Bruce
ANTARTICA Sir James Clark Ross
AUSTRALIA John MacDouall Stuart
CANADA Sir Alexander MacKenzie
EUROPE James Boswell

POLITICS

Arthur James Balfour
Andrew Bonar-Law
George Brown
Sir Henry Campbell-Bannerman
James Keir Hardie
Alexander Douglas Home (Lord Home)
James Ramsey MacDonald
Sir John Alexander MacDonald
Lord Reith
Emmanuel (Manny) Shinwell (Lord Shinwell)
John Smith
Viscount William Whitelaw

ARCHITECTURE, ART & DESIGN

Robert Adam
Sir William Arrol
Henry Raeburn
Allan Ramsay
Charles Rennie Mackintosh

VISUAL ARTS

Ken Currie
Adrian Wiszniewski
Peter Howson
Eduardo Paolozzi

SPORT

Matt Busby (football)
Willie Carson (horse racing)
Jim Clark   (motor racing)
Kenny Dalglish (football/commentary)
Sir John Sholto Douglas, 8th Marquis of
   Queensbury (devised the Queensbury
   Rules for boxing)
Gavin Hastings (rugby)
Benny Lynch (boxing)
Eric Liddell (running)
Catriona Matthew (golf)
Ally McCoist (football)
Peter Nicol (squash)
Richard Noble (world land speed record holder)
Jackie Stewart (motor racing)

TELEVISION

Rory Bremner
Muriel Gray
Gregor Fisher
Lorraine Kelly
John Sessions
Alastair Sim
Elaine C. Smith
Kirsty Wark
Richard Wilson

CINEMA

Robert Carlyle
Sean Connery
Billy Connolly
Tom Conti
Ewan MacGregor
David Niven
Bill Forsyth (director and filmmaker)

MUSIC (Classical / Opera)

Evelyn Glennie
Lisa Milne
James MacMillan

MUSIC (Celtic)

Ally Bain
Archie Fisher
Niel Gow
Karen Mathieson
Ian Wallace

MUSIC   (Rock & Pop)

Bay City Rollers
Del Amitri
Sheena Easton
Annie Lennox
Lulu
Donnie Munro
Marti Pellow
Eddi Reader

LITERATURE

Iain Banks
Sir J(ames) M(atthew) Barrie
James Boswell
John Buchan (Baron Tweedsmuir)
Robert Burns
Sir Arthur Conan Doyle
Alasdair Gray
Janice Galloway
Kenneth Grahame
Lewis Grassic Gibbon (James Leslie Mitchell)
Neil Gunn
Liz Lochhead
Sir Walter Scott
Muriel Spark
Robert Louis Stevenson
Irvine Welsh

suggested further reading

Keith Aitken — *The Bairns o' Adam: the story of the STUC* — Polygon 1997

Bernie, Brand & Mitchell — *How Scotland Votes* — Manchester University Press 1997

Angus Calder — *Revolving Culture: Notes from the Scottish Republic* — I.B. Taurus 1993

Alan Clements, Kenny Farquarson & Kirsty Wark — *Restless Nation* — Mainstream, 1996

Gordon Donaldson — *Scotland's History: Approaches and Reflections* — Scottish Academic Press 1995

Donnachie & Whatley (Ed.) — *The Manufacture of Scottish History* — Polygon 1992

Dudley Edwards — *A Claim of Right for Scotland* — Polygon 1989

Jeff Fallow — *Old Scotland New Scotland* — Luath 1998

Richard J. Finlay — *Independent and Free* — John Donald 1994

Alexander Grant — *Independence & Nationhood* — Edinburgh University Press 1991

Alasdair Gray — *Why Scots Should Rule Scotland* — Canongate 1997

James Halliday — *Scotland - a Concise History* — Gordon Wright 1996

Christopher Harvie — *Scotland and Nationalism* — Routledge 1994

John & Julia Keay (Ed.) — *Collins Encyclopaedia of Scotland* — HarperCollins 1994

Michael Lynch   *Scotland: A New History*
Pimlico 1992

Seamus Mac A'Ghobhainn & Peter Beresford Ellis   *The Scottish Insurrection of 1820*
Pluto 1989

Iain MacDougall   *Labour in Scotland*
Mainstream 1985

Fitzroy MacLean   *Scotland - a Concise History*
Thames & Hudson 1993

McCrone, Morris & Kelly   *Scotland the brand - the making of Scottish heritage*
Edinburgh University Press 1995

Nan Milton   *John MacLean*
Pluto, n.d.

James Mitchell   *Strategies for Self - Government*
Polygon 1995

Rosalind Mitchison   *Why Scottish History Matters*
Saltire Society 1997

Lindsay Paterson   *The Autonomy of Modern Scotland*
Edinburgh University Press 1994

John Prebble   *The Lion in the North*
Penguin 1981

Paul H. Scott   *Towards Independence*
Polygon 1991

Peter & Fiona Somerset Fry   *The History of Scotland*
Routledge 1982

The Scottish Office   *Scotland's Parliament*
1997

T.C. Smout   *A Century of the Scottish People*
Fontana 1987

Tom Steel   *Scotland's Story*
Fontana 1985

Kenyon Wright   *The People say Yes*
Argyll 1997

index

Jeff Fallow is a freelance illustrator and graphic designer living in Fife. He is also the author and illustrator of **Wales for Beginners**™ *and illustrator of* **London for Beginners**™ *and a political cartoonist, with work published in* CND TODAY *and* SCOTS INDEPENDENT.